Video Analysis of Authentic Teaching

Video Analysis of Authentic Teaching

A Resource Guide for Professional Development and Growth

Edited by
Carrie Eunyoung Hong
and Irene Van Riper

ROWMAN & LITTLEFIELD
Lanham • Boulder • New York • London

Published by Rowman & Littlefield
An imprint of The Rowman & Littlefield Publishing Group, Inc.
4501 Forbes Boulevard, Suite 200, Lanham, Maryland 20706
www.rowman.com

6 Tinworth Street, London SE11 5AL, United Kingdom

Copyright © 2019 by Carrie Eunyoung Hong and Irene Van Riper

All rights reserved. No part of this book may be reproduced in any form or by any electronic or mechanical means, including information storage and retrieval systems, without written permission from the publisher, except by a reviewer who may quote passages in a review.

British Library Cataloguing in Publication Information Available

Library of Congress Cataloging-in-Publication Data

Names: Hong, Carrie Eunyoung, editor. | Van Riper, Irene, 1947- editor.
Title: Video analysis of authentic teaching : a resource guide for professional development and growth / edited by Carrie Eunyoung Hong and Irene Van Riper.
Description: Lanham, Maryland : Rowman & Littlefield, 2019. | Includes bibliographical references and index.
Identifiers: LCCN 2018056378 (print) | LCCN 2019003610 (ebook) |
  ISBN 9781475832174 (electronic) | ISBN 9781475832150 (cloth : alk. paper) |
  ISBN 9781475832167 (pbk. : alk. paper)
Subjects: LCSH: Teachers—In-service training—Audio-visual aids. | Teachers—Training of—Audio-visual aids. | Video tapes in education. | Teacher effectiveness.
Classification: LCC LB1731 (ebook) | LCC LB1731 .V45 2019 (print) |
  DDC 370.71/1—dc23
LC record available at https://lccn.loc.gov/2018056378

∞™ The paper used in this publication meets the minimum requirements of American National Standard for Information Sciences—Permanence of Paper for Printed Library Materials, ANSI/NISO Z39.48-1992.

This book is dedicated to all preK–12 teachers and school personnel who make a difference in the lives of children. The commitments of these educators to improve education and strengthen the teaching profession are greatly appreciated.

This book is dedicated to my family for their endless support and encouragement.

—*C. E. H.*

Thank you to every teacher who has taught in the classrooms of the world. You are to be revered and admired. You are the change agents who develop and support our children.

This book is dedicated to my family and colleagues who have supported me throughout my career.

—*I. V. R.*

Contents

Preface		ix
Acknowledgments		xi
Introduction		xiii
1	Video Analysis for Professional Development	1
	Carrie E. Hong and Irene Van Riper	
	Defining Video Analysis	2
	Implementation of Video Analysis	5
	Recommendations	10
	Key Contents	11
	References	12
2	Strategies for Administrators and Teachers	13
	Irene Van Riper, Carrie E. Hong, and Joan Roman	
	Looking at Video Recording through Various Lenses	13
	Video-Based Professional Development	16
	Video Clubs	17
	Other Types of Video-Based Professional Learning	18
	Observation of Authentic Classroom Events	19
	Reflective Practices	20
	Instructional Strategies	20
	Key Contents	22
	References	22
3	Video-Based Reflection of Teaching	25
	Michelle Gonzalez and Carrie E. Hong	
	Defining Reflection	26

	Benefits of Video	30
	Shift of Focus to Student Performance	33
	Student-Centered Reflection	34
	Benefits of Video-Based Reflection	36
	Barriers to Reflection	38
	Key Contents	40
	References	40
4	Deepening Teacher Learning with Video Clubs	43
	Carrie E. Hong and Irene Van Riper	
	Video Analysis in Advancing Pedagogy	44
	Professional Abilities of Video Analysis	45
	The Study	47
	Teachers' Varied Abilities in Video Analysis	52
	Benefits and Challenges of Video Clubs	54
	Key Contents	55
	References	55
5	Online Video Sharing for Teacher Assessment	57
	Alex Chambers	
	Streaming Video	57
	Technical Requirements	60
	Software Options	62
	Feedback Options	66
	Conclusion	68
	Key Contents	69
	References	69

Appendix A	71
Index	73
About the Contributors	75
About the Editors	77

Preface

Today, in the sphere of rating teachers for merit, the spotlight is on teacher reflection and evaluation. It seems that programs for teacher preparation are remiss in equipping pre-service teachers with the technological tools to implement a regular schedule for self-analysis. The focus is on implementing strategies, but there is a strong need to scaffold the ways in which teachers can look objectively and without criticism at themselves.

Employing video recording snippets of an instructional day provide teachers with the opportunity to study themselves as professionals interacting with children. In their jam-packed day of teaching content and engaging in formative assessments, teachers rarely have the time to reflect on how that day progressed.

Analyzing video of one's teaching of and interaction with students offers a peek into the effect of pedagogical choices and how students are processing the information. It is a view into how the classroom looks to an objective observer. If seen alone, or in collaboration, a video of the classroom offers a rich context from which to study and understand the complex interactions that occur.

If students are not on task, or behaving inappropriately for the environment, a video review can help teachers figure out why a certain student is not attending to the material. It can provide answers to difficult questions about off-task behavior. If a student continuously raises his or her hand to respond to the teacher and is often overlooked, a teacher who is unaware of this can correct that moving forward. Video reflection and analysis can offer teachers and colleagues the impetus to begin conversations about what happens in the classroom—the very situations that impact every student every day.

This book was compiled to support in-service teachers to refine their pedagogy, focus on their students' learning, become aware of the classroom environment, develop their understanding of interactions and behaviors, and identify problems and potential problems. The outcome of video reflection, hopefully, is a change or tweaking of pedagogy to encourage content mastery and a fuller conception of one's classroom environment.

Teachers must be so much more than instructors. Administrators and parents expect teachers to consider learning styles, pacing of lessons, and differentiation and individualized instruction of all students. We owe teachers a clear and systematic method to support their reflections and analyze that data to strengthen their instructional style.

Acknowledgments

We would like to thank the chapter authors for their contributions, and we are grateful for their exemplary work and passion in improving teacher learning. This book could not have been written without their professional expertise.

We are deeply indebted to Joe Van Riper who helped us edit and format this work and are grateful for his technical expertise and strong support.

Finally, we acknowledge the fine support from the team at Rowman & Littlefield.

Introduction

We live in a world of constant changes in media and technology. Among the many educational tools used in preK–12 schools, video technology provides new possibilities of collaborative learning between teachers and educational personnel and serves as a medium of professional development. This volume offers conceptual frameworks, strategies, and practical suggestions to implement video-based professional development programs in preK–12 schools.

Video offers many benefits as a learning tool for teacher development and professional growth. For example, classroom videos provide a common ground for teachers to understand effective strategies for meeting the specific needs of students. Actions and behaviors observed in video serve as a set of rich data to account for student learning and engagement.

This book comprises five chapters. Each chapter addresses a distinct topic that targets a slightly different audience. Readers may select a specific chapter of their interest or navigate among chapters.

Chapter 1 provides a research review on the effects of video analysis for teachers' professional development. A conceptual framework based on the literature helps teacher educators and school leaders understand and learn research-based strategies to maximize the benefits of video. Reviewing the characteristics of effective video-based professional development programs, readers can adapt best practices when they establish a video-based professional learning community.

Chapter 2 provides strategies for administrators and teachers in using video recording as a resource to reflect on and evaluate instruction. If video is used as an evaluation tool, the establishment of mutual trust and collaboration is imperative. The chapter shares voices and viewpoints of administrators and teachers when it comes to watching and sharing videos of classroom instruction.

Chapter 3 engages in-service teachers in discussions about the benefits of video-based reflection. The chapter shares a case study of video-based reflection in a graduate course. Teachers had an opportunity to watch their own instructional video clips and reflect on their practice to remediate students' literacy needs. The chapter emphasizes the different levels and depths of reflection that teachers may experience as their pedagogical knowledge and practice are expanded and enriched.

Chapter 4 highlights video clubs as a professional learning tool. Based on a pilot study, the chapter introduces how video clubs promote a rich discussion about teaching and learning. The chapter discusses benefits and challenges in using video clubs among teachers and other school personnel.

Chapter 5 provides an overview of the research, technical requirements, strategies, and best practices for using a video-streaming platform via a video-sharing website for providing feedback to in-service teachers. The chapter discusses strategies and technical requirements for sharing videos for assessment and evaluation purposes. The chapter emphasizes the benefits of establishing a system of video sharing to assess in-service teacher knowledge and to provide feedback.

Chapter 1

Video Analysis for Professional Development

Carrie E. Hong and Irene Van Riper

Today's schools are changing rapidly with concurrent educational reforms and technological advances. The scope of educational technology is getting wider and more varied than ever before. Video technology, in particular, is at the center of heightened attention because it provides valuable learning opportunities for practicing teachers.

Advances in digital videography, video-analysis software, and online tools have led to an increased use of video in teacher education and professional development. Videos provide easier access to classroom teaching and learning. Video recording of authentic classroom events can serve as an anchor for collaborative discussions among members of professional-learning communities. It is also considered a potentially powerful learning tool for advancing teacher knowledge and skills.

Despite the growing use of video technology in the field, there is surprisingly little awareness or training to help teachers effectively use and critically analyze video recordings of classroom instruction for their professional growth. Video-based professional development programs, such as video clubs, are a relatively new concept, although the use of video itself has existed in educational fields for some time.

This chapter will provide readers with an overview of literature regarding the use of video analysis for teachers' professional development. It will also help readers build a conceptual framework to support effective video analysis for the purpose of teacher growth. A review of current literature is included to help readers learn research-based strategies for maximizing the benefits of video analysis.

The characteristics of effective video analysis recommended in this chapter may serve as a model for teacher educators and school administrators as they implement video-based professional development in various contexts.

DEFINING VIDEO ANALYSIS

In video analysis, videos become an integral part of the program for teachers' professional development. The use of videos makes it easier for teachers with diverse backgrounds to reach a common ground and discuss educational issues with the goal of meeting specific student needs in authentic and relevant ways. Also, the analysis of authentic teaching and learning promotes an in-depth knowledge of instructional practices.

Unlike the real-time observations of classroom teaching, video analysis affords collaborative discussions among teachers and has the potential to promote teacher learning by exchanging constructive feedback regarding each other's instruction. Videos provide concrete examples and evidence to which teachers may refer. Moreover, analyzing other teachers' videos can help teachers expand their professional expertise and extend their understanding to practices beyond the classroom.

There are several ways of using video in teacher education. Specifically, video analysis is an activity in which teachers review recordings of authentic classroom events. During video analysis, teachers are expected to make active connections to their own teaching by activating prior knowledge and experience and then engage in analytic activities either individually or collaboratively.

Video analysis is often used to facilitate active learning in pre-service or novice teachers regarding *what* and *how to teach*. Additionally, it is used as a tool for in-service teachers to improve their professional practice. Research demonstrates that the main objectives of video analysis in professional development are to:

a. analyze the diversity of classroom practices,
b. stimulate professional reflection,
c. coach with various teaching strategies in a complex learning context, and
d. evaluate teacher competencies for specific issues.
   (Gaudin and Chaliès 2015)

A group of teacher educators designed and implemented video-based training for practicing teachers in a graduate literacy course. Through trial and error they discovered that to achieve the desired effects in teacher development, there was a need for sufficient knowledge and experience about video analysis. They learned that for any video-based reflection to be effective careful planning and systemic implementation is required.

These teacher educators found that it is important to embrace flexibility in the process of the design and implementation of video analysis to maximize growth in teacher learning. Videos are only effective when their use is clearly aligned with learning objectives. The value of a video is determined by the way in which it is used.

There is a consensus in research that video-based reflection is a valuable activity that fosters teacher learning (Sherin and van Es 2009; Tripp and Rich 2012; Zhang, Lundeberg, Koehler, and Eberhardt 2011).

Video Analysis in Practice

Using a specific example, you can see what video analysis looked like when it was used in a teacher education course. In a graduate-level literacy methods course, a group of special education teachers with various teaching backgrounds watched a seven-minute clip of a literacy lesson taught by an unknown reading teacher.

The clip featured one of the lessons taught to two struggling readers who were in first grade. The lesson was designed for use in a small-group reading intervention. As seen in the clip, the reading teacher, trained to be a state reading specialist, modeled for her students how to retell a story by using a retelling rope. This is a hands-on prop specifically designed to help students recite story elements.

After being provided with contextual information of the students and the intervention plan, the group of special education teachers shared what they observed in terms of effectiveness regarding the instructional strategies that were used to meet the students' needs.

A few experienced teachers in the group activated their prior knowledge and experience of working with beginning readers with similar needs. Using their current teaching experience, elementary teachers shared what they thought were effective strategies for beginning readers, whereas, the middle and high school teachers in the group contributed their analysis of instructional strategies that may have worked for older students with similar reading difficulties.

In this example, a topic of the collaborative discussion began with what had been observed in the video clip. Then, the pattern of the group discussion gradually shifted to include each teacher's reflection on the topic and connections to their own teaching context.

The video clip definitely initiated teachers' thinking about instructional strategies for retelling, in particular. It then prompted teachers to engage in a conversation about retelling strategies across different contexts with various groups of students.

To sum up, a group of special education teachers had an opportunity to engage in a focused discussion of how to teach retelling strategies to a diverse group of students. A video recording of a reading teacher's lesson served as a springboard for ensuing and richer discussions.

Teachers' Thinking during Video Analysis

Videos can aid reflection on teaching and learning. Observing a recording demonstrating other teachers' instruction is a secondhand experience. However, it is an engaging activity if teachers can make connections to their own practices and achieve a deeper level of engagement. While watching videos of other teachers, viewers may realize that the teachers in the videos face issues similar to those in their own classroom.

Video analysis provides an opportunity to make meaningful connections among professionals. Authentic classroom events are a rich source of data that can spark teachers' problem solving in an authentic way. This authenticity, in turn, positively impacts teaching and learning (Shanahan and Tochelli 2014). Effective instruction is enriched by what teachers do in practice with their knowledge.

Video analysis can engage teachers in active learning experiences. Videos stimulate teachers' cognition and provide motivation to reflect on the teachers' current practices. These teachers may be stimulated to make changes in future instruction. Specifically, video analysis requires cognitive demands by viewers to *observe*, *identify*, and *interpret* classroom events, although the nature of analysis is dependent on objectives and learning goals.

Observation of Lessons

Unlike the traditional methods of on-site classroom observation, video technology affords repeated viewing of the same lesson. This feature is often used to help teachers participate in a deeper analysis of one specific event out of many that occurred in the lesson. Also, the same clip can be watched multiple times from multiple perspectives.

Videos have the benefit of overcoming the limitations of memory-based reflection. Rosaen, Lundeberg, Cooper, Fritzen, and Terpstra (2010) assert that reviewing one's own video helps a teacher fill in the gaps between what is retained from memory and what is actually observed in the video. They went on to suggest that analyzing one's own video provides concrete evidence of changes in practice.

Identification of Relevant Events

When watching a video of their own lesson, most teachers do not distribute their attention equally between every instance and every behavior of both the teacher and the students. Research has found that a teachers' ability to notice relevant events varies (Seidel, Stürmer, Blomberg, Kobarg, and Schwindt 2011). This ability does not correlate with their teaching experience but is more directed by their experience with, and practice of, video analysis.

With training, teachers become more conscious of noticing relevant events for a purposeful reflection. For example, Rosaen, Lundeberg, Cooper, Fritzen, and Terpstra (2008) found that prior knowledge and experience in video analysis has a positive effect on video-based teacher learning.

Practice-to-notice means learning to pay attention to what is important or what is relevant. It helps teachers make connections between classroom interactions and broader educational contexts. Using what they know about the context and the students, teachers are capable of applying comparisons to what and how they teach according to learning goals and student needs (van Es and Sherin 2002).

Interpretation of Classroom Interactions

Once teachers are able to identify relevant evidence in the video, it is important for them to interpret classroom interactions with their knowledge and reasoning. A video is an effective tool to help teachers reflect on their instruction. Reviewing recordings of their own teaching provides an opportunity for teachers to "stop and think" during their busy schedule in school. This is the time when teachers can make meaning of classroom interactions and plan for future instruction.

To take advantage of video-based reflection, teachers need to be comfortable with watching themselves in a video. It is likely that teachers may feel awkward analyzing one's own teaching, but with practice, they will begin to shift their attention from their own instruction to the students' performance. Videos provide teachers with an opportunity to review how students learn.

IMPLEMENTATION OF VIDEO ANALYSIS

There are many components to be considered when implementing video analysis for teacher learning. What are the types of video material, analytic activities, settings for individual or collaborative analysis, evaluation of learning goals, and so on?

Research shows that a range of design and implementation approaches have been used in various programs for video-based professional development, but the effects of video analysis also depend on the learning goals and characteristics of the participating teachers. One should pay particular attention to:

a. types of video material,
b. analytic activities that teachers engage in, and
c. evaluation of video analysis for teacher development.

Types of Classroom Videos

The nature of classroom videos, viewed in the context of professional development, determines the objectives or characteristics of programs for video-based professional development. Gaudin and Charliès (2015) identified three types of videos frequently used in teacher training:

a. classroom videos of unknown teachers,
b. classroom videos of peers, and
c. classroom videos of one's own teaching.

Video examples of both effective and ineffective teaching practices can be used. Even videos of ordinary classroom lessons have value in promoting teacher learning. Teachers may watch published or edited selections of classroom events to find new ideas or to review an exemplary lesson. Unedited footage of classroom lessons also serves as "raw" data for open-ended analysis, depending on learning objectives.

As teachers bring their knowledge into practice during video analysis, viewing one's own teaching and comparing it with others' results in different effects on teacher learning. In many cases of video-based professional development, teachers have empathized with one another and realized that other teachers have similar issues (Borko, Jacobs, Eiteljorg, and Pittman 2008).

It is more likely that experienced teachers are very willing to criticize their own lessons, but their analysis is rarely as critical when discussing videos of their colleagues. And yet, experienced teachers are eager to suggest helpful alternatives to the lessons of teachers less experienced than they are. One may ask then, *does it matter whether teachers watch videos of their own teaching or that of others?*

Kleinknecht and Schneider (2013) used a quasi-experimental approach to examine the effects of specific types of video on teachers' emotional and motivational processes. The results of the study show that positive emotional and motivational effects were noticed when teachers analyzed videos of their own instruction; however, the observation of other teachers' videos led to deeper reflection on negatively perceived events in the video.

They concluded that video analysis of one's own and other teachers' videos leads to different effects on teachers' cognition, motivation, and emotion. The study recommends that programs for video-based professional development should be designed to align learning goals with appropriate types of video material.

Other research reported similar results, indicating that teachers become more engaged in analytic activities when they view videos of unknown teachers rather than videos of their peers or colleagues (Seidel et al. 2011). This is because teachers feel more comfortable with analyzing the instruction of unknown teachers rather than that of their peers.

Positive effects from video analysis on viewers' self-reflection, and changes in their own instruction are not always guaranteed (Gaudin and Chaliès 2015). Teachers are more likely to reflect on their instruction when they analyze a video of themselves because it provokes an emotional response. Once teachers get used to viewing their own videos, they become increasingly motivated to make changes in their instruction (Siedel et al. 2011).

Research recommends that teachers have a full understanding of classroom events, as well as, general contexts of teaching and learning when they watch videos of unknown teachers. Otherwise, their analysis is constrained only by what is observed through the lens of the camera.

It is also recommended that teachers begin their video analysis by working with videos of their own teaching. This facilitates the activation of prior knowledge and experience regarding teaching and learning. With experience, this activation of relevant knowledge and experience helps teachers analyze videos of unknown teachers on similar topics.

Effects of Different Types of Videos

Zhang et al. (2011) examined the effects of three types of videos on teacher learning: published videos, teachers' own videos, and peers' videos. The study suggests that each type of video has a unique value in terms of affordances and challenges in enhancing teacher reflection on practices.

Consider the responses of one teacher who participated in a program of professional development. In this program, a group of teachers watched and discussed lessons of various types of video material. This study summarized affordances and challenges of each type of video for the focus teacher, Emma.

Emma, a novice kindergarten teacher, had two years of teaching experience. A published video helped Emma learn about the problem-based learning approach, refine her research plan, and expand her knowledge of pedagogical models. The major drawback of the published video was Emma's lack of contextual understanding, which limited her ability to actively participate in video analysis.

When watching a video of her own teaching, Emma had difficulty articulating the lens through which she analyzed her lesson. Teachers in the video-analysis group tended to provide positive feedback for Emma, whose video was viewed and discussed. By observing and discussing videos of other teachers in her group, Emma was able to adopt and incorporate the strategies she observed into her own teaching.

As described in Emma's case (Zhang et al. 2011), it is important to select appropriate types of video and use them productively to meet the learning objectives of video-based programs of professional development. The following questions will guide readers when selecting the types of video for teacher learning.

- Within the current learning context, what are the benefits and challenges related to each type of video (e.g., published, unedited, unknown teachers, peers, or one's own)?
- Which type of video material is most appropriate for participating teachers to learn from?
- What is the rationale of selecting specific types of video to achieve the learning goals?

Analytic Activities

A video can be used as a springboard to prompt productive discussions about teaching and learning. Video analysis of exemplary lessons has a different impact on teacher learning than does the analysis of typical classroom events. Videos of exemplary lessons can provide teachers with new knowledge and skills, whereas videos of regular lessons may serve as a springboard for collaborative discussion among viewers.

In some contexts, a video clip of another teacher's lesson can serve as practice for observing one's own. To make video-analysis effective, establishing an exemplary analysis process is more important than using videos of exemplary lessons.

Once the types of video material are determined, the following questions can be raised to help determine what types of activities the teachers will engage in.

- In what ways will teachers engage in video analysis (e.g., will they view clips individually or analyze the clips in group)?
- How will teachers analyze the selected videos (e.g., will they share with peers verbally, or write their analysis first)?
- What kind of focus, if any, should be emphasized (e.g., should the focus be placed on teacher, students, lesson objectives, assessment, or something else)?

Specific activities or behaviors that take place during video analysis are vital to determining the objectives of video-based teacher training. Analytic activities are the ones that stimulate cognitive, emotional, and motivational processes in teachers. Unless specific guidance is provided by facilitators or experts, teachers will typically produce a range of responses to the same classroom event.

Research suggests that teachers' engagement in video analysis is a gradual progression of distinct but interrelated cognitive activities, from activating *selective attention* to *knowledge-based reasoning* (Sherin 2007; Sherin and van Es 2009). The progression of teachers' perceptual processes takes place in three levels (Seidel et al. 2011).

At the first level, teachers notice classroom events and are able to describe what is happening in the video with varying degrees of details. Teachers need to know, out of many instances occurring in a classroom, what is worth paying attention to and what is not. If there is no guidance provided by experts, some teachers may lack the ability to select relevant events that may lead to a critical analysis of their instruction.

Selective attention is a strategic method for avoiding superficial or unproductive observation of classroom events. Teachers can learn and activate selective attention with the guidance of experts and repeated practice. With increased experience in video analysis, teachers gain the ability to distribute their attention purposefully to achieve productive outcomes.

At the second level, teachers move beyond simply identifying or describing what has occurred in a classroom and are able to provide reasoning for why they occurred. Research shows that teachers typically pay attention to their own behavior when viewing videos of their teaching. This teacher-centered attention also happens when videos of unknown teachers are used. However, with guidance and practice, teachers can shift their attention to student performance and learning.

With this shift, teachers' analysis becomes centered on the students and based on evidence. For example, teachers use specific examples and evidence observed in the video to explain classroom interactions. At this level, experienced teachers or experts see relationships among lesson plans, instructional methods, and student learning in ways that novices may not (Brunvand 2010).

At the third level, based on what is identified in the video, teachers apply what they have learned in terms of their instruction and student learning to future lessons. Unlike novice teachers, experienced teachers are capable of correlating what has been noticed in the video with their knowledge of content and pedagogy.

Teachers use *knowledge-based reasoning* to suggest instructional changes based on student needs. With the practice of video analysis, teachers can articulate what changes should be made and what kinds of instructional strategies would be appropriate to improve student learning.

Evaluation of Video Analysis

How do we know that teacher learning has improved? There is limited research on systemic assessment of video-based programs of professional development. The following questions, based on Santagata's (2014) model, provide insights on how to assess the effects of video analysis:

- What were the learning objectives and outcomes of using video?
- Was the selected video material appropriate to achieve the learning goals?
- Did the viewing modality (individually or in group) serve that purpose?
- What kinds of data sources can be used to assess the ways in which videos affect teacher learning (e.g., written reflection, survey or questionnaire, checklist for changes in teacher knowledge and practice)?

To maximize the benefits of video analysis, it is important to assess the extent to which video analysis helps teachers develop a reflective and analytic mind-set. This means "learning to reason systematically based on evidence and knowledge of students' learning and curricular issues in that domain" (Sherin 2004, 14).

The use of video evidence provides potential for enhancing teacher learning. Because video serves as a tool for teacher development by which teachers engage in reflective practice and make changes to their future practices, evaluation must focus on growth of teacher knowledge and changes in teacher instruction.

RECOMMENDATIONS

Effective use of videos in professional development includes three components: learning goals, instructional approaches, and video materials (Kleinknecht and Schneider 2013). The program must be developed to include a clear learning goal with an evaluation plan for teacher learning.

The level of experience that participating teachers have with video-based analysis must be considered in determining an instructional approach. For instance, if participants are beginning teachers, the guidance of experts needs to be provided. If teachers are familiar with video analysis, expert facilitation can be replaced with a learning community in which participants establish mutual trust and collaboration.

Several suggestions to consider when using videos for teacher learning include:

1. To reduce the cognitive load on teachers with limited experience in video analysis, short clips, of a minimum of three to five minutes can be used so participating teachers become familiar with what is expected during video analysis. Teachers can watch the clips individually and engage in collaborative analysis with peers. As viewers grow more familiar with the

learning context of the video, productive discussions may lead to a deeper level of analysis.
2. Providing explicit prompts is an effective way to promote productive discussions. If the group consists of both experienced and less-experienced teachers, prompts will help teachers find a common ground. When viewers have no or minimal experience of video analysis, either focused prompts or a facilitator's role is crucial to engage viewers in the practice of noticing relevant events. Although videos may capture the richness and complexity of classroom interactions, a facilitator is needed to encourage viewers to look beyond the obvious.
3. To avoid the dichotomy of good-versus-bad practices, it is important to choose clips that do not necessarily depict totally effective or ineffective practices. The advantage of using relatively ordinary lessons is that teachers can focus on, and practice, the analytic process without making judgments. For example, teachers may feel detached when they watch published videos that are edited to feature "noticeable" moments of the lesson. In the same manner, when teachers watch a clip of a lesson that is not as effective, more experienced teachers may only find errors and suggest alternatives.
4. Readers must capitalize on the potential of videos in professional development with innovative methods. Little is known or researched in terms of effective protocols for video-based programs of professional development (Gaudin and Charliès 2015). The use of videos in education is receiving increased attention because of its great potential for sustained teacher development and the establishment of professional-learning communities. By taking advantage of technological advances, teacher–leaders and teacher–educators are encouraged to explore innovative methods in the design and implementation of video analysis.

Finally, we would like to remind readers that the use of video is a technological tool. Its value is determined by the ways in which it is used. Videos have both benefits and limitations, so it is imperative to be critical about their effectiveness.

KEY CONTENTS

- Definition of video analysis
- Conceptual framework for video analysis
- Review of research on video analysis
- Recommendations for video-based programs of professional development

REFERENCES

Borko, H., Jacobs, J., Eiteljorg, E., and Pittman, M. E. (2008). Video as a tool for fostering productive discussions in mathematics professional development. *Teaching and Teacher Education, 24*(2), 417–36.

Brunvand, S. (2010). Best practices for producing video content for teacher education. *Contemporary Issues in Technology and Teacher Education, 10*(2), 247–56.

Gaudin, G., and Charliès, S. (2015). Video viewing in teacher education and professional development: A literature review. *Educational Research Review, 16*, 41–67.

Kleinknecht, M., and Schneider, J. (2013). What do teachers think and feel when analyzing videos of themselves and other teachers teaching? *Teaching and Teacher Education, 33*, 13–23.

Rosaen, C. L., Lundeberg, M., Cooper, M., Fritzen, A., and Terpstra, M. (2008). Noticing noticing: How does investigation of video records change how teachers reflect on their experiences? *Journal of Teacher Education, 59*(4), 347–60.

Rosaen, C. L., Lundeberg, M., Cooper, M., Fritzen, A., and Terpstra, M. (2010). Interns' use of video cases to problematize their practice: Crash, burn, and (maybe) learn. *Journal of Technology and Teacher Education, 18*(3), 459–88.

Santagata, R. (2014). Video and teacher learning: Key questions, tools, and assessments guiding research and practice. *Beiträge zur Lehrerbildung, 32*(2), 196–209.

Seidel, T., Stürmer, K., Blomberg, G., Kobarg, M., and Schwindt, K. (2011). Teacher learning from analysis of videotaped classroom situations: Does it make a difference whether teachers observe their own teaching or that of others? *Teaching and Teacher Education, 27*, 259–67.

Shanahan, L., E. and Tochelli, A. L. (2014). Examining the use of video study groups for developing literacy pedagogical content knowledge of critical elements of strategy instruction with elementary teachers. *Literacy Research and Instruction, 53*, 1–24. doi: 10.1080/19388071.2013.827764.

Sherin, M. G. (2004). New perspectives on the role of video in teacher education. In J. Brophy (Ed.), *Using video in teacher education, advances in research on teaching*. Vol. 10 (1–28). New York: Elsevier.

Sherin, M. G. (2007). The development of teachers' professional vision in video clubs. In R. Goldman, R. Pea, B. Barron, and S. J. Derry (Eds.), *Video research in the learning sciences* (383–95). Mahwah, NJ: Lawrence Erlbaum.

Sherin, M. G., and van Es, E. A. (2009). Effects of video club participation on teachers' professional vision. *Journal of Teacher Education, 60*(1), 20–37.

Tripp, T. R., and Rich, P. J. (2012). The influence of video analysis on the process of teacher change. *Teaching and Teacher Education, 28*, 728–39.

van Es, E. A., and Sherin, M. G. (2002). Learning to notice: Scaffolding new teachers' interpretations of classroom interactions. *Journal of Technology and Teacher Education, 10*(4), 571–96.

Zhang, M., Lundeberg M., Koehler, M. J., and Eberhardt, J. (2011). Understanding affordances and challenges of three types of video for teacher professional development. *Teaching and Teacher Education, 27*(2), 454–62.

Chapter 2

Strategies for Administrators and Teachers

Irene Van Riper, Carrie E. Hong, and Joan Roman

Teachers today are inundated with state and federal regulations, curricula decisions, counseling children and parents, differentiated instruction, and school parameters. It is expected that they follow the vision and mission of the school and observe the written and unwritten manuals of the operations of their administration.

Teachers must learn to be intentionally reflective in their choice of pedagogy and demonstrate an awareness of the level of their students' mastery of knowledge. Many teachers and administrators find that video recording a few minutes of activity in the classroom or part of a lesson is helpful in maintaining consistent understanding of what happens in the classroom.

Technology can assist teachers in improving their instruction and student learning in numerous ways. Video can serve as a reflective tool in any learning context. Classroom videos in particular are a rich source of data with many talking points for teachers and educational personnel across grade levels and subjects.

In this chapter, we will present research-based strategies for administrators and teachers who would like to use video technology in their evaluation and reflection of instructional practice.

LOOKING AT VIDEO RECORDING THROUGH VARIOUS LENSES

According to the reflection of a football coach, teachers and administrators can benefit from the implementation of video recording to "improve teaching techniques" (Cross 2012). Sports coaches have been using video recordings for many years to observe plays, skills, and players.

Although Cross (2012) reports athletics and classroom teaching are quite different, the use of video recording is a beneficial tool to help teachers and athletes improve and become motivated. There are specific guidelines for using video recording in sports that can easily be translated into the classroom (Cross 2012).

If a teacher's concern is that students are not mastering an important concept, then a video recording might help identify the unforeseen reason. A quick video recording from a mobile device can give the teacher the ability to watch the video as many times as needed to determine the problems in the classroom.

Teacher and student commentary can be tagged to study the way information is being processed. Parents, teachers, and administrators can view the recording together.

All participants can reflect on the video and offer commentary or suggestions. This video might be designated as an anchor video, with each skill and strategy demonstrating best practices in the classroom. Expectations are front-loaded to ensure that the teacher knows what must be demonstrated in the classroom; there is no ambiguity.

Just as the coach looks at the video through a sports lens, the teacher is able to see the classroom and students through an academic lens to strengthen pedagogy. In fact, the teacher can record the video and request that the administrator view the video and help to identify any skills or strategies that might have gone unnoticed by the teacher.

Here is a review of the use of video recording from the viewpoints of administrators and teachers.

Administrator Viewpoint

Administrators, who have employed video recording in their teacher observations, discussed the various ways in which they used video recordings to reflect on and strengthen teacher excellence in the classroom. One administrator reported that both teacher and administrator agreed to video record an activity or lesson to fulfill the administrator's task of observing and appraising the teacher.

The teacher and administrator decided on a specific time frame to be recorded. The two planned to meet after the observation, watch the recording together, and discuss it. They agreed that this was to be reflective and analytical, not a criticism of the teacher or pedagogy.

The administrator and the teacher offered questions and thoughts that evolved into a collaborative brainstorming session. Queries presented were:

- When you put your students in small groups, have you considered what happens when you go from one group to another?
- What are your impressions of the engagement of the students?
- What do you see?

The responses of the teacher included, "I wasn't aware that I did that," "I didn't see that one of the students had his head down on his desk," and "I didn't realize I called on the same students all the time." Teachers often observed that they were not allowing time for students to process information or that they were not circulating around the room to be certain that all students were on task.

When one teacher refused to video record lessons, the administrator felt that it was because of a lack of trust and belonging. It is critical, added the administrator, to build that level of relational capacity with the teaching staff so they feel secure in analyzing their own classroom techniques and asking for support when needed. The administrator can assure the teacher that the video is not used for criticism, but as an opportunity for personal and professional growth.

Thus, it is imperative for the administrators to be well prepared for video analysis and reflection. In a later section of this chapter, several considerations are listed for administrators to keep in mind as they implement video-based teacher evaluations.

Teacher Viewpoint

Setting up a video camera in a class is a daunting task for some teachers. Once the recording is done, watching oneself on video is not always an easy task. Teachers may feel awkward after watching their first video. It takes courage for them to get out of their comfort zone and become more comfortable with watching themselves on video.

There are also concerns if the video is shared with others. Teachers may think that they are exposing themselves to the judgment and scrutiny of others. If a teacher agrees with the power of reviewing her or his instruction on the video, the use of video for professional growth takes time and effort for any teacher.

After watching her first video, Jessica, a fourth-grade teacher, commented that the short video recording of her instruction had increased her awareness of classroom activity. She also stated that her reflective practice had been enriched by studying the video recording because she was able to view the social interaction of her students as well as the academic aspects of her lesson. Another fourth-grade teacher, Danielle, wrote after watching recorded videos of other teachers:

> I think watching the videos helps show examples in a practical way. As a visual learner, I appreciate when the information is presented in a visual way, especially when I see a teacher conducting the theory in the classroom. It makes the information more concrete for me.

When teachers are confident that they know what is expected in their classroom, they understand the benefit of video recording their lesson or activity. After watching and reflecting on their own behavior in the classroom, teachers should easily be able to recall the theory-to-practice principle. In some contexts, a video clip of other teachers' lessons can serve as practice on how to observe one's own video.

According to Tripp and Rich (2012), teachers' self-reflection of their video recordings can support improved pedagogy by using several strategies to facilitate the experience. Tripp and Rich (2012) offer six dimensions that scaffold the viewing and reflection process. Detailed questions are unpacked to provide helpful guidelines for the teacher who may feel overwhelmed by this process.

These dimensions look at complexities such as specific tasks, guided reflection, individual or collaborative reflection, length of video to be reviewed, number of reflections needed for the task to be of benefit, and the methodology for assessment. Teachers, who are new to video analysis or evade it because of the ambiguity of the process, are now able to engage in viewing their pedagogy using an outline of guiding questions.

VIDEO-BASED PROFESSIONAL DEVELOPMENT

Research highlights that a common goal of using video analysis for teachers' professional development is to become *adaptive experts* in education. Through reflective analysis of instruction, the use of video can assist teachers in expanding "the breadth and depth of their experience and knowledge about teaching, both of which can be applied to new contexts" (Rosaen, Carlisle, Mihocko, Melnick, and Johnson 2013, 170).

Unlike the use of video analysis to teach pedagogical knowledge and skills for initial teacher preparation programs, video analysis for practicing teachers must focus on teachers' advanced knowledge and skills to meet diverse student needs (Polly and Hannafin, 2011).

While watching classroom interactions, teachers gain a deeper and broader understanding of the relationship between their instruction and students' performance. This analytic activity can enhance teachers' adaptive expertise.

Recording authentic classroom events provides a set of data with which to review a complexity of elusive classroom practices, such as tacit interactions between student and teacher and student to student. Students' behaviors, that are not obvious to the teacher when he or she is engaged in instruction, become clear while viewing a video playback of classroom events.

Tripp and Rich (2012, 729) summed up benefits of video reported in relevant studies. Video helped teachers to:

a. identify gaps between their beliefs about good teaching and their actual teaching practices;
b. articulate their tacit assumptions and purposes about teaching and learning;
c. notice things about teaching that they did not remember (from memory);
d. focus their reflections on multiple aspects of classroom teaching; and
e. assess the strengths and weaknesses of their teaching.

Video is widely used in professional-learning communities where teachers explore issues of teaching and learning specific to their classrooms in a safe and collaborative setting. As a result, video-based professional programs have been initiated and implemented in some schools, although types and objectives of such programs vary across schools. In this chapter, we will examine benefits of video clubs and other types of video-based professional learning among teachers.

VIDEO CLUBS

There is an increased interest in using video as a tool for professional development. Video clubs are well known for helping practicing teachers build the capacity to notice and interpret specific classroom events. Within a format of video clubs, teachers can form a study group in which a group of teachers analyze videos of classroom practice.

Van Es and Sherin (2010, 155) defined a video club as "a professional development environment in which groups of teachers watch and discuss excerpts of videos from each other's classrooms." Video clubs can be formed to review each other's videos and exchange ideas and feedback. Moreover, members of a video club can discuss specific topics from watching different types of video, such as published or unknown teachers' lessons.

Video clubs, as a form of professional-learning community, are effective because teachers experience the benefit of providing mutual support for each other. Watching the same video clip and sharing individual observations opens up the possibility of seeing classroom interactions from multiple perspectives. This learning opportunity affords a discussion around instructional strategies to serve diverse learners.

Research found that a discourse pattern visible within settings of a video club suggests that teachers pay close attention to students in the video rather than the teacher's actions (van Es and Sherin 2006, 2008). Collaborators in video clubs that bring teachers together for a sole purpose should not only include a discussion of teaching practices, but also the analysis of student thinking as viewed in the lesson (van Es 2012).

When teachers understand what and how students think, they become aware of the cognitive processes that are switched on as students digest information. As a result, video clubs promote not only an analysis of teacher pedagogy, but also a clearer view of student information processing (van Es 2012). Teachers are then able to design lessons that are tailored to the multiple cognitive needs of their students.

Shanahan and Tochelli (2014) explored the participation of nine elementary teachers during discussions of a video study group in which teachers had opportunities to investigate their pedagogical content knowledge needed for explicit strategy instruction. Findings of the study suggest that engaging in video study groups afforded teachers opportunities to reason their pedagogical moves based on students' needs.

A format of video clubs or video-based study groups shows promise as a tool for increasing teachers' use of explicit strategy instruction because teachers had ample opportunities to bring their "tacit knowledge to a more explicit level by obtaining feedback and exploring their conceptualization" (Shanahan and Tochelli 2014, 20).

OTHER TYPES OF VIDEO-BASED PROFESSIONAL LEARNING

A study reported that the use of brief instructional video clips has great potential to enhance collaborative insights within the school community (Sterrett, Dikkers, and Parker 2014).

Researchers worked with two elementary schools to examine the impact of video as a tool for facilitating communication, reflection, and collaboration within the school setting. At faculty meetings of each school, short video clips of the lessons taught by one of the teachers in the school are shared to encourage dialogue and collaboration among faculty.

The school's principals and teachers perceived this video-based professional development in a positive way. Specifically, the teachers recognized the value of video in seeing new ideas and strategies in practice. The principals thought that the video-based staff development promoted a culture of finding experts within the school.

Professional development for faculty is beneficial only if the quality of the session is relatable to the teachers. Polly and Hannafin (2011) report on learner-centered professional development stating that professional development for teachers must follow the pedagogy teachers employ in their classroom. It must be tailored to the situation and the needs of the learner.

Like their students, teachers benefit most from professional development if they are permitted to extend the learning to their own classroom. This practice would allow them the opportunity to use the knowledge and skills imparted (Polly and Hannafin 2011). The structure of this type of professional development is important for teachers as they begin to implement the new skills and strategies within the construct of their unique classroom.

Video Analysis for Professional Learning

Video analysis is beneficial in improving professional learning. When teachers and administrators watch video through an analytic lens, they engage in a cognitively demanding thinking process by applying their professional knowledge and experience. Video analysis can be used to improve a specific set of professional skills. Three components of video analysis determine effectiveness of video-based professional development:

a. observing authentic classroom events,
b. guided practice for critical analysis, and
c. reflection and changes in practice.

Using a set of authentic classroom events on video is an effective way to engage teachers in video analysis. Teachers become more involved when they can relate to what is shown in the video. Experienced teachers trained in video analysis can play a facilitator role by keeping discussions focused and monitoring learning progress.

Prompts or questions for viewers to focus on and address are always helpful in getting conversations rolling. Guided practice of video analysis supports teachers' in-depth reflection on instruction and promotes further changes in practice.

OBSERVATION OF
AUTHENTIC CLASSROOM EVENTS

The learning goals of video analysis will determine whether teachers observe recordings of either their own instruction or the practices of other teachers. If the purpose of the video analysis is centered on reflection and changes in practice, analyzing a teacher's own recording leads to direct impact on future lessons. If the objectives of video analysis require teachers' cognitive engagement, watching recordings of others affords an analytic evaluation of what has been observed.

Experiences of analyzing and discussing recorded classroom lessons help teachers see patterns of activity and draw inferences about student learning. Guided practice of video observation or analysis is crucial in bringing positive changes to teaching and learning. It is important to set learning goals before one engages in video analysis.

Depending on the length of the video clips, optimal effectiveness varies. Research recommends a minimum of two- to seven-minute clips if a collaborative discussion is planned after watching the clips. Characteristics of clips may depend on the learning objectives of video-based professional development.

REFLECTIVE PRACTICES

Specific activities or behaviors that take place during the video analysis are key objectives of video-based reflection. Analytic activities compel teachers to engage in cognitive, emotional, and motivational processes.

Consider now this specific example of video analysis among practicing teachers across different grade levels. Teachers watched a series of video lessons taught by unknown teachers and were asked to reflect on the benefits they got out of the video.

One teacher wrote, "I enjoy watching good teachers teach and hope to get ideas that I can implement in my classroom situation." Another teacher described the benefits of watching video as a learning tool that she can easily relate to.

> I think watching these pre-recorded videos allows me, as a visual learner, to see approaches I can use hands on in my own classroom, and what these approaches look like. I think sometimes you read about what works in a book but visually seeing it modeled by another teacher is a whole other level of learning.

Teacher self- reflection of authentic classroom videos frames strong practice in the classroom and fosters teacher growth. It supports teachers in understanding the complexities of their pedagogical practice and the way in which their students are receiving and using the information. It is a trajectory for collaboration: teacher to teacher, teacher to administrator, and teacher to student.

INSTRUCTIONAL STRATEGIES

Seidel, Stürmer, Blomberg, Kobarg, and Schwindt (2011) reports that for strategic video instruction to be most effective, there must be a universal understanding of the targeted skill. The study looks at two different types of modules for video instruction: example-rule and rule-example. If linking foundational study to pedagogy is the objective, it must be clearly stated, so that teachers understand the purpose of the activity.

Although this research of Seidel et al. (2011) highlights pre-service teachers, the conclusions derived connect to in-service teachers as well. The scope and depth of knowledge regarding real classroom experiences, "the rule-example" module, promotes evaluation of classroom situations (Seidel et al. 2011).

The use of video modeling and recording in the "rule-example" modules embedded in coursework allows for the teacher to extract an understanding of the importance of lesson planning and differentiated instruction, among other contextual factors.

Use of Video to Improve Teaching for All Teachers

The broad strokes benefit of video recording is exhibited in the instruction of music teachers. Denenburg (2015) offers methods used in music classes for teachers to hone their pedagogy. Music teachers record, evaluate, and revisit their lessons, both in the classroom and the private studio.

The feedback and discourse of ideas and advice is invaluable for improvement of the implementation of strategies. Teachers develop skills and understand the complexities of their classroom dynamics.

A teacher–educator or administrator might share a link to a video they have recorded to spark a rich discussion and to model video concepts. Self-improvement and reflective evaluation are the main goals. A written analysis guided by a rubric should accompany the video recording. The teacher–educator or administrator is then able to watch the video aligned with the self-analysis and offer beneficial commentary.

In another study (Osipova, Prichard, Boardman, Kiely, and Carroll 2011), video is implemented to study the efficacy of instruction in elementary special education reading. In-service teachers use video recording as a self-reflective tool to enable them to study their practice of teaching how language works when they teach word study and fluency in students with learning disabilities.

In the study, teachers watched video recordings of their own instructional practice throughout the school year and reflected on them by examining what worked and offering suggestions of what might enhance their practice. Osipova et al. (2011) concluded that reflective teachers, who are able to determine problems in their practice, are empowered to reframe these problems in the service of finding solutions to improve their pedagogy.

Recommendations for School Community

Video analysis should be reflective and outlined, offering specific and detailed strategies to teachers so that they have scaffolding and questions for structured viewing. The questions provided should be tailored to the teacher's classroom situation, which are different for math, music, athletics, and special education environments. If we agree that every student is unique, we must also believe that every teacher has specific needs as well.

Forging connections for collaborative reflection is essential to developing a program in the school community. A planned time that is carved out for the purpose of a collaborative study should be in place so that it is unrushed and scheduled into the school calendar.

Teachers may reflect individually, or within a safe and comfortable group, after viewing a snippet of a video. Questions for analysis should be in place to benefit the growth and enrichment of pedagogy and to capture a better and more informed understanding of the cognitive development of students within that classroom.

Video analysis is a tool that can be implemented in a variety of educational settings: in a program for teacher preparation for the improvement of graduate students (Cahalan 2013), in an evaluative discussion with educational leaders, and in professional development. Consideration of teachers' beliefs and feelings regarding video analysis is of the utmost importance in the implementation process in the school community.

KEY CONTENTS

- Viewpoints of administrators and teachers
- Video-based professional development
- Use of video for all teachers
- Recommendations for school community

REFERENCES

Cahalan, J. (2013). Teaching classroom video recording analysis to graduate student: Strategies for observation and improvement. *College Teaching, 61*, 44–50.

Cross, N. (2012). How the football coach can help principals and teachers score. *The Phi Delta Kappan, 94*(2), 58–61.

Denenburg, M. (2015). Using video recording to improve your teaching. *Clavier Companion,* (July–August), 11–13.

Osipova, A., Prichard, B., Boardman, A. G., Kiely, M. T., and Carroll, P. E. (2011). Refocusing the lens: Enhancing elementary special education reading instruction through video self-reflection. *Learning Disabilities Research and Practice, 26*(3), 158–71.

Polly D., and Hannafin, M. (2011). Examining how learner-centered professional development influences teachers' espoused and enacted practices. *The Journal of Educational Research, 104,* 120–30.

Rosaen, C. L., Carlisle, J. F., Mihocko, E., Melnick, A., and Johnson, J. (2013). Teachers learning from analysis of other teachers' reading lessons. *Teaching and Teacher Education, 35,* 170–84.

Shanahan, L. E., and Tochelli, A. L. (2014). Examining the use of video study groups for developing literacy pedagogical content knowledge of critical elements of strategy instruction with elementary teachers. *Literacy Research and Instruction, 53*(1), 1–24.

Seidel, T., Stürmer, K., Blomberg, G., Kobarg, M., and Schwindt, K. (2011). Teacher learning from analysis of videotaped classroom situations: Does it make a difference whether teachers observe their own teaching or that of others? *Teaching and Teacher Education, 27,* 259–67.

Sterrett, W., Dikkers, A. G., and Parker, M. (2014). Using brief instructional video clips to foster communication, reflection, and collaboration in schools. *The Educational Forum, 78,* 263–74. doi: 10.1080/00131725.2014.912370

Tripp, T. R., and Rich, P. J. (2012). The influence of video analysis on the process of teacher change. *Teaching and Teacher Education, 28,* 728–39.

van Es, E. A., and Sherin, M. G. (2006). How different video club designs support teachers in "learning to notice." *Journal of Computing in Teacher education, 22*(4), 125–35.

van Es, E. A., and Sherin, M. G. (2008). Mathematics teachers' "learning to notice" in the context of a video club. *Teaching and Teacher Education, 24*(2), 244–76.

van Es, E. A., and Sherin, M. G. (2010). The influence of video clubs on teachers' thinking and practice. *Journal of Math Teacher Education, 13,* 155–76. doi: 10.1007/s10857-009-9130-3.

van Es, E. A. (2012). Using video to collaborate around problems of practice. *Teacher Education Quarterly,* (Spring), 103–16.

Chapter 3

Video-Based Reflection of Teaching

Michelle Gonzalez and Carrie E. Hong

The use of reflection in education is common and considered a best practice to help develop the teaching practice of pre-service, novice, and expert teachers. Not only is reflection a common practice in education today, but it is also a necessary practice in teacher education and professional development. Simply put, reflection is central to the life of an educator (van Manen 1995) and commonly accepted as a central principle of the learning and teaching processes (Zeichner and Liston 1987).

However, reflection has not always been a prominent practice in the field of education. Reflection grew to prominence in the 1980s after the publication of Schon's (1983) work and the discontent with the oversimplistic and technical perception of education (Sparks-Langer and Colton 1991). Often the focus for educators was on "doing" rather than on "thinking" (Hatton and Smith 1995).

Likewise, before the movement toward the use of regular reflection, the focus in education was on training teachers in certain behaviors. The alternative for teachers could have been thinking about the reasons and rationales associated with different teaching practices and growing their abilities to make informed decisions in their teaching practices.

Such decisions would have been based on the teachers' goals; the contexts of the classroom, school, and community; and the needs of their students (Zeichner 2008). Being an educator is a complex and multifaceted professional process, and in addition to being a science, it can be considered an "art" as well. To effectively perform as an educator, reflection is an essential piece.

This chapter engages readers in discussions about how teachers can benefit from video-based reflection on their own instruction. During clinical practice of reading remediation courses designed for practicing teachers to be certified as reading specialists, teachers had an opportunity to view their own instructional video clips and reflect on their practice to remediate the literacy needs of K–12 students.

Specifically, the chapter provides an overview of the benefits of video-based reflection by examining the ways that teachers reflect on their literacy instruction. This is done from reviewing recorded videos showing their teaching of students with learning difficulties.

DEFINING REFLECTION

Though reflection is an everyday necessary exercise for practicing teachers, it is difficult to define. Terms such as *reflection, reflective thought, critical reflection, reflective practitioner,* and *reflective thinking* are often all used interchangeably.

John Dewey, a US philosopher, was perhaps the first educator to attempt to define reflection. He is often credited as being the founder of reflective practice. A noteworthy definition of reflection comes from his work. Dewey (1933, 9) states:

> Active, persistent, and careful consideration of any belief or supposed form of knowledge in the light of the grounds that support it, and the further conclusions to which it tends, constitutes reflective thought. . . . It is a conscious and voluntary effort to establish belief upon a firm basis of reasons.

In other words, reflection is a thoughtful and conscious process that leads to informed judgment and decision making. For this reason, reflective terms (i.e., reflective thought, critical reflection, reflective teaching, etc.) as defined and used in teacher education are not as important as the process of reflection, the content of the reflection, and the effects of reflection on teacher practice.

Types of Reflection

Rather than defining reflection, other scholars have attempted to identify the key types of reflective thinking. The key types of reflective thinking can be examined in the context or time when they occur. Schon (1983) delineated reflection into two components: *reflection in action* and *reflection on action*.

Reflection in action occurs during instruction and is central to professional teaching practice (Schon 1983). Though essential, it may be the most difficult type of reflection (van Manen 1991) because it requires the teacher to "think (reflect) on his or her feet," make an informed decision, and then take action. Teachers are constantly using reflection in action throughout the school day to help make instructional and procedural decisions in the moment.

Reflection in the moment or in action is limited to the task at hand rather than the possibilities such as the different layers of interpretation, multiple ideas for next steps, and even possible consequences (van Manen 1995). This type of reflection is addressed as *reflection on action*. Reflection on action takes place after the instruction has occurred and is typically what in-service teachers do daily after lessons.

For example, as a practicing teacher, Jessica's long commute to and from her school is when most of her best reflection on action is done! This long commute is the perfect time in her busy work schedule for reflecting on teaching.

During reflection on action, she evaluated the successfulness of her lessons and thought about whether changes she made during the lesson (using reflection in action) could have resulted in different outcomes. The reflection on action is an opportunity for classroom teachers, like Jessica, to reflect on what they would do next in their lessons.

Van Manen's Stages of Reflection

Reflection on action can be viewed in stages through which both the novice and more experienced teacher progress. Expert teachers progress further through the reflective stages and reflect more critically and analytically. This is because they have much deeper and richer schema from which to draw when reflecting and reaching conclusions, in comparison with novice teachers (Sparks-Langer and Colton 1991).

Thus, it is expected that expert teachers may be further along the continuum of reflection. Van Manen (1977) developed a three-level framework for understanding the development of reflection in teachers. He believed that as teachers' self-efficacy increased, their reflective practice would be enhanced, which correlates with the ideas that a tenured teacher may reflect on a deeper level.

The first stage (Level 1) that van Manen (1977) identified is *technical rationality*. In this level, educators provide only a description of what happened, and the focus is on teacher behavior. The occurrences in the classroom are not viewed as a problem, and no connections are made to theories or systems. An example of a Level-1 reflection can be taken from journal writing in which teachers reflect on their literacy instruction from memory. In the following example, an in-service teacher, Kelly, is reflecting on the use of graphic organizers with second-grade students.

> Brian and Justin were present for the first half of this mini-lesson. Both boys referenced the story elements graphic organizer as we read so that we could work together to fill in the details. The students raised their hands as I read when they heard information that we were looking for (characters, setting, problem, etc.).

This example shows a teacher is simply reporting on what happened during the literacy lesson with no analytical thought or problem identification.

The second reflection stage (Level 2), *practical action*, extends from Level 1. Elements from Level 1 may be present, but now the teacher identifies a problem and suggests an alternative solution to the problem. This new alternative would most likely be implemented by the teacher. Then, the teacher describes the outcome and suggests further modifications to be implemented.

Again, this level can be illustrated in an example from teachers' memory-based reflection. The same teacher, described previously, is reflecting on the use of graphic organizers by her students. This time, she takes her reflection a step further by identifying a problem and presenting a solution. In her reflective journal, she wrote:

> Each boy was able to fill in the five sections of the graphic organizer independently. They did refer to the vowel sounds and words we previously practiced to help with their spelling and were able to come up with all the information for their chart independently. After I modeled the transition from graphic organizer to a written piece the boys were all able to do the same. I did explain and remind the students to use punctuation marks at the end of each idea. I also reminded them that each box on the graphic organizer was a spot for one idea, so they represented when to use punctuations as well.
>
> The final products show that all three boys need support in applying capitalization and punctuations. In the future, I will work with them to edit previously created sentences, so they learn where and why these details are important. At some point this will transition to the boys writing sentences and later more short pieces before tracing all capitals and punctuations in blue to promote checking their work for these important components.

In this journal excerpt, the teacher begins in the Level 1 reflective stage by stating what occurred within the lesson. However, she then transitions to the second level by identifying a problem: her students are not using punctuation and capitalization. She then identified a solution; editing sentences that would be implemented in the next session. She even identifies what she will work on after editing the sentences.

The third stage (Level 3), *critical reflection*, builds on the first and second levels, but at this stage, the teacher considers ethics (such as appropriately educating English-language learners) and approaches the reflection with an open mind. The teacher in this stage also considers the moral and ethical implications of his or her teaching. This third level is sometimes called *critical reflection* (Sparks-Langer and Colton 1991).

Van Manen's third stage is more difficult to reach. Often, teachers remain stagnant at the second level. To be able to reach the level of critical reflections, teachers need guidance and tools to assist them in reflecting more deeply about their practices. It is believed that the use and analysis of video-recorded lessons can guide teachers to this third level.

The use of video-based reflection allows teachers to expand their reflections beyond what occurred in the lesson to the implications of the lesson. Therefore, it is likely that the third level of reflection occurs after a teacher reviews and reflects upon her or his recorded lessons.

For example, Amanda, an elementary teacher, was working with first-grade bilingual students at a university-based reading clinic to improve their phonemic awareness and phonics skills. She was using strategies similar to the ones she had been using in her classroom of first graders.

After viewing her recorded lesson, she reflected on and wrote in a reflective journal why these students in the clinic were having difficulty acquiring these skills. She was questioning if the strategies she was using were appropriate because of the students' language needs.

This example illustrates the third level of reflection because Amanda is questioning the appropriateness of the strategies used. Her concern was based on the bilingual status of her students in the clinic.

She also maintained an open mind by considering that perhaps the same strategies she was using in her current classroom were not appropriate with the students in the reading clinic. She worried about the different characteristics between the students in her classroom and those she tutored in the clinic. She recognized that the bilingual students had a unique need, and she was willing to research appropriate strategies for this population.

A more critical reflection went beyond just identifying a problem and its solution. She was careful to consider moral and ethical factors in the process. This level of reflection could lead to a more effective or appropriate solution than if the teacher had simply stopped at the second level of reflection.

It appears that Amanda was able to move from Level 2 to Level 3 in her reflections because of the assistance of the recorded clinic video she viewed after each remediation session. Viewing the video allowed her to reflect on and identify things that she did not notice during the lesson. It also permitted her to look more closely at specific parts of her lesson, which would most likely not have been possible had she merely relied on her memory of the lesson while writing the reflection.

Using Video to Reflect

Reflective teaching is a key component in advancing teachers' professional knowledge and skills. Reflection on one's own instruction is a well-known practice for professional development because reflection leads teachers to a greater and more thorough understanding of their students' strengths and needs (Scales 2012). Deep knowledge of one's students can lead to positive changes in instruction and practice (Jaeger 2013).

For the same reason, teachers' professional abilities to evaluate evidence of student performance and the effectiveness of their instruction in meeting specific needs are vital components of effective teaching (Danielson 2013). A teacher's actions in monitoring student learning can be accomplished with active and conscious reflection in action (Schon 1983).

However, in reality, time is generally too limited for teachers to focus on all student activities as well as their own interactions with students. Reflection on action is required for teachers to observe classroom events they had missed during the actual lesson and to expand their attention to other issues of teaching and learning.

BENEFITS OF VIDEO

The use of video has long been used to improve teacher learning. As a result of recent technological advances, video is widely used in a variety of programs for professional development employing various approaches in design and implementation. Videos recently became an integral part of professional-learning communities within K–12 schools (Sterrett, Dikkers, and Parker 2014).

For example, teacher video clubs are now as popular as other forms of learning communities, such as study groups or inquiry groups. While sharing video clips of their lessons with peers, members of the video club explore issues of teaching and learning specific to their classrooms in a safe and supportive environment (van Es 2012).

Research has shown that teacher learning is effective when teachers discuss issues directly related to their own teaching experiences and student needs (Seidel, Stürmer, Blomberg, Kobarg, and Schwindt 2011). Professional development is even more effective if teachers examine their own authentic teaching through systematic practices of reflective teaching (Tripp and Rich 2012).

Therefore, the use of video has a great deal of potential to enhance teachers' instruction because it affords teachers the opportunity to reflect on their practices in a specific context and in an authentic way.

Using recordings of their own teaching, teachers can afford expanding their foci of reflection to include multiple aspects of teaching, such as classroom interactions and subtle details of student performance. In addition, advanced video technology offers various tools to enhance all types of teacher reflection before, during, and after lessons, both in and out of the school setting.

Specifically, advances in digital recording and convenient file sharing on various electronic devices makes it easier than ever for teachers to reflect on their teaching. Most recently, a range of video-analysis software that assists a systematic and collaborative analysis of instructional video among teachers is a contributing factor for the active use of video within schools as well as in programs for professional development (Rich and Tripp 2011).

Teachers' self-analysis of their videos provides them a unique opportunity. The teacher is able to have a close look at student learning and the specifics of student performance that might have been unnoticed during the lesson. Video-based reflection encourages teachers to pay close attention to learners, and it helps teachers enhance the pedagogical knowledge they used to meet the various needs of student learning (Shanahan and Tochelli 2014).

Likewise, studies of video analysis highlight that teachers can evaluate their instruction and make changes in their instructional strategies as a result of video analysis of student learning and progress (Tripp and Rich 2012).

For instance, based on a meta-analysis of the seven experimental studies that examined the effects of video analysis on teacher change, Nagro and Cornelius (2013) concluded that video analysis is a tool for teacher development to promote positive changes in teaching and ultimately to enhance student learning. They indicate that video analysis can assist both "internal changes in teacher reflection and external changes in teacher practice" (2013, 315).

Video Analysis

In recent years, video-based reflection has steadily received scholarly attention in the field of teacher education. Several studies have reported that the focus of teachers' reflections changed when they participated in video-based analysis of their instruction (e.g., Christ, Arya, and Chiu 2012; Rosaen, Carlisle, Mihocko, Melnick, and Johnson 2013; Siedel et al. 2011; Zhang, Lundeberg, Koehler, and Eberhardt 2011).

In these studies, teachers were able to observe relevant learning aspects and were more effective in analyzing student performance than when they reflected on their lesson from memory. However, simply watching one's own video does not bring about changes in teaching. A systematic analysis of teaching and student learning based on critical reflection is required to affect instructional practice.

Teachers can use video analysis to assess the extent to which their lesson has advanced students' knowledge and skills. For example, while replaying their recorded lesson, teachers can analyze student actions and responses so that they can accurately assess student understanding of the lesson.

Video analysis is a highly effective tool with which teachers may develop a reflective and analytic mind-set involving "selective attention" and "knowledge-based reasoning" (Seidel et al. 2011, 260–61). *Selective attention* means that teachers examine specific examples and scenes out of the various activities that took place in the video for an analytic purpose.

During video analysis, teachers are encouraged to not only evaluate the relationship between their instruction and student learning, but also to justify their future instruction based on student performance and learning outcomes observed in the video.

If effectively implemented, video analysis helps teachers learn "to reason systematically based on evidence and knowledge of students' learning and curricular issues" (Rosaen et al. 2013, 171). Knowledge-based reasoning is an evaluative and reflective practice in which teachers can activate their professional knowledge and make connections between their instructional strategies and student-learning outcomes. This reasoning process addresses teachers' professional abilities to link theory with practice (van Es 2010).

During video analysis, teachers' awareness of student performance begins with an act of noticing (van Es and Sherin 2010). Noticing requires refocusing teachers' attention on classroom events and student behaviors that they had missed or did not remember. It would be difficult to remember certain aspects of their teaching and student reactions based *only* on memory. The use of video is an effective tool for finding concrete evidence of student learning because it provides an opportunity to view the specific actions of classroom events.

However, teachers need guidance and practice to maximize the benefits of video analysis. Objectives of video analysis must focus on the teachers' increased ability to notice relevant evidence of student learning, to interpret classroom interactions, and to evaluate the relationship between instructional practices and student achievement.

Research also shows that teachers' experience and practice with video-based reflection is correlated with the effectiveness of video analysis for professional growth (Kleinknecht and Schneider 2013). Rosaen et al. (2013) suggest that expert teachers see relationships among lesson plans, instructional methods, and students' learning in ways that novice teachers do not. Guidance and scaffolding with a clear purpose and focused analysis is a critical component of video-based reflection.

Expert guidance serves to direct teachers' attention to certain aspects of teacher instruction and student learning. Purposeful prompts can help teachers activate their pedagogical knowledge and promote higher-order thinking, such as analyzing classroom events within a broad learning context and justifying future instruction to address specific learning needs.

For this reason, most literature on video analysis suggests that guided video analysis is more productive than open-ended analysis of instructional videos (Baecher and Tuten 2011; Marsh, Mitchell, and Adamczyk 2009).

Video-Based Reflection of Teacher Instruction

Case studies are provided here of two teachers who relied on video recordings of their lessons to reflect on their instruction of struggling readers.

These students were enrolled in a reading clinic in the northeastern part of the United States. The reading clinic is a university-based facility that offers reading remediation for local public school students in grades K–12.

Each clinic room is equipped with a video camera to record clinic sessions. Recordings are immediately available for playback via a password-protected website. Also, the video playback platform allows teachers to employ time stamps and write brief descriptions or commentary.

On this same campus, university faculty members taught a practicum course within a graduate-level program for reading specialists. The graduate students in the course, who were mostly practicing teachers, had the opportunity to design and implement literacy remediation programs based on assessment data they gathered in a previous semester. As course requirements, each clinic session was video recorded. Teachers were told to watch their videos and annotate the recorded sessions by activities using time stamps.

Teachers were required to write a commentary for each area of literacy needs that was addressed in the lesson. Based on the review of their recorded teaching, teachers wrote a commentary responding to suggested categories, such as:

a. analyzing student performance,
b. assessing student learning, and
c. using their analysis to inform instruction.

SHIFT OF FOCUS TO STUDENT PERFORMANCE

Nicole is a certified English language arts teacher enrolled in a graduate-level certification program for reading specialists. She tutored Alexis, a fourth-grade student, at the reading clinic. At the beginning of the clinic, Nicole expressed her reluctance to watch herself teaching, as did most teachers in the course. However, as the clinic progressed, Nicole became one of those who actively used the video recordings to reflect on her instruction.

A salient pattern of difference in her reflections is related to shifts in her attention to what took place in the video. She appeared to become more perceptive of student performance as her clinic sessions progressed.

For example, in her annotations of the first remediation session, Nicole wrote,

> Alexis was asked to read the vocabulary words out loud, and make a prediction on what the text might be about based upon the words taken out of the context of the reading passage. Alexis made a valid prediction. Alexis made connections to the words by giving me various examples and putting the words into sentences.

She also commented,

> I created a graphic organizer to help Alexis organize her thoughts while closely viewing the media clip. Alexis struggled with the term *viewpoints*. Alexis knew the words *pro* and *con*, but struggled to put evidence into the appropriate columns.

The pattern of her observations during the first couple of sessions focused mainly on procedural aspects of her lesson. This focus shifted after she analyzed four more sessions with Alexis. Nicole's video annotations of the later sessions demonstrate that she paid more frequent attention to student performance than on instructional procedures. Her observation of student behaviors became more specific, using concrete examples of the student's needs.

> The phrase "losing ground" confused Alexis. This is another indicator that she gets confused with common English phrases. . . . Alexis re-read the article and extracted pros and cons about school year-round. Alexis stopped after two sentences were read and questioned the text to monitor her comprehension of the text.

This shift of teacher attention was also observed in her written commentary, which was completed after she reviewed and annotated her video. She wrote:

> Alexis had no difficulty working with the words previously pulled out from the context of the reading passage. Alexis is still having some difficulty conceptualizing the terms *economic*, *academic*, and *socialization*. Alexis'[s] explanation is loose, which is an indication that she is not fully grasping the idea of what the economy is and how it impacts the topic of school year-round and her personally.

Nicole experienced growth in her video reflections by especially paying close attention to student performance and analyzing strengths and needs of the student. This was true not only for Nicole, but also for most teachers who reviewed and annotated the video recordings. They demonstrated a similar shift in their attention to a more focused, specific, and interpretive analysis of student performance.

STUDENT-CENTERED REFLECTION

The following case is based on Elaine, who worked at the clinic with three second-grade students, or clients, (Josh, Oscar, and Manny). Elaine is a certified elementary teacher, teaching second grade in a local school district. Josh and Manny had diagnoses of dyslexia. After studying her video analyses, a few interesting themes emerged, which will be discussed along with examples.

The first theme that emerged, while analyzing Elaine's video reflections, was that she remained student-centered in her video reflections throughout the clinic sessions. This was a surprise. The prediction was that the early reflections would mostly be centered on the teacher because Elaine focused mainly on her own behavior in the clinic.

However, Elaine was a veteran teacher, which may have contributed to her continual focus on the client in the video reflections. The following example illustrates how Elaine's reflections remained centered on the students.

> Josh built a sentence with all necessary components, and Manny was able to listen to the sentence and identify the who and the what.

A second important theme that emerged was a shift in Elaine's reflections from being oriented on the students as a group to being oriented on the students as individuals. There was a noticeable shift from reflections directed toward the group of three clients to specifically focusing on each one individually. Early in the semester, Elaine also had difficulty differentiating her clinic lesson plans for each client, and this was reflected in her video analyses.

As the semester progressed, she improved in seeing and understanding more clearly the individual needs and abilities of each of her clients. For instance, in her video reflection for the first clinic session, nine of her twelve reflections focused on all of the clients as a group, whereas in her final video reflection only three of her thirteen reflections focused on the entire group.

The following example illustrates how she focused her reflections on the group, and the second example illustrates how she began making reflections for each client individually.

> The clients were able to take their previously organized ideas and write them in the format of a short piece. I was impressed with their attention and stamina as we finished this task in literally the final minutes of our session.

> While the boys read independently it was clear Oscar was reading because he often whispered the story and asked for help a couple of times. As time went on Josh stopped using his finger to follow along and I could tell his eyes were drawn to the illustrations and not the words. I offered to help him and he didn't accept my offer until Oscar had asked for help a couple times. Manny struggled to read sight words as well as many other cvc and cvce words were in his text. He also had a difficult time staying focused while conversations were going on with the two other students about their texts.

Another theme was observed as Elaine began to analyze the sessions more deeply and began to reflect on why the clients were exhibiting particular behaviors. In an early reflection, Elaine wrote:

> The boys shared their opinions (favorite color) through questioning to support understanding of what an opinion is, as there were a couple misconceptions about this concept.

In this example, Elaine is simply stating what the boys did and that they had some difficulties. A second example, written at the end of the semester, illustrates how Elaine's reflections developed.

> Oscar's puzzle pieces were incomplete because he was missing the ending punctuation. Not only was he unsure of whether to use a question mark or period, he could not understand how to turn the rectangular piece to make the puzzle fit. It is an incredible simple puzzle, so this caused me to question his visual perception and ability to analyze images.

Overall, it is thought that Elaine exhibited growth in her video reflections, especially in the area of analyzing each client as an individual, which possibly illustrates her increased knowledge of each student and their strengths and needs. Her reflections essentially became more centered on the students as the semester progressed.

BENEFITS OF VIDEO-BASED REFLECTION

There is no doubt that reflection will not be eliminated from educational programs. Nor will it fall from the daily routines of practicing educators because of the benefits it provides in advancing the teaching practices of all educators at different points in their careers. Most notably, reflection leads to professional growth. Dewey (1933) was early to recognize the power of reflection, believing that reflective practice could lead to change and professional growth.

Later, Schon (1983) articulated that reflection in action is the key to professional development in educators. More recently, Scales (2012) asserted that reflective practice leads to professional learning. Corcoran and Leahy (2003) insist that teachers must include reflection in their work to maintain professional growth.

The previously discussed benefits are present in both traditional and video-based reflections. However, a powerful argument can be made that the use of video can more easily assist educators to reach the critical stage of reflection. This will be explored in depth next.

The use of video in reflection, again, allows educators to reflect more deeply and move through van Manen's (1977) three levels of reflection. Specifically, it is believed that the use of video can assist the educator in moving from the first level (technical rationality) to the second level (practical action) of reflection, and that with guidance, educators can move from the second level to the third level (critical reflection).

Van Manen's third level of reflection should be a worthy goal of educators because it allows them to reflect beyond the technical aspects of their jobs, such as teaching skills and strategies.

Instead, critical reflection allows educators to reflect on the ends (policy) of education, the moral and ethical considerations of teaching, and the social conditions of education (Zeichner 2008). These are areas that teachers do not often reflect on, but they are important because it could lead to change in policy by teachers themselves rather than bureaucrats.

Van Manen's (1977) third level requires the educator to approach the reflection with an open mind and without bias. The use of video allows this approach to occur. Traditional reflective practice relies on memory. In the traditional method, educators base their reflections on what they thought or perceived they saw, heard, and so on. But the use of video provides concrete evidence concerning what happened during the lesson.

Though there is still a level of perception and interpretation in the use of video, educators can get a clearer picture of what occurred in the lesson. Less time is spent remembering what occurred and more time can be spent on thinking about why things occurred, as well as the moral, ethical, and social considerations of education.

The movement through van Manen's (1977) first two levels with the assistance of video is evident in the previous two case studies of Nicole and Elaine. Both teachers had either limited or no experience in using video as a tool for reflection.

Both teachers started in van Manen's first level of reflection, technical rationality, where they primarily focused on their own teaching behavior. They then progressed to the second stage, practical action, where reflections became more centered on the students and oriented on problems.

It was demonstrated that the use of video allowed Nicole and Elaine to focus more on student performance and less on their behavior. It allowed them to notice more student behavior (reaction to lesson and student learning) and use selective attention of student behavior.

This is important because the focus on student behavior allowed Nicole and Elaine to understand the strengths and needs of their students more deeply, which progressed to more student-tailored remediation lessons. Ultimately, more exact or pinpointed remediation lessons should lead to improved student outcomes.

It should be noted that Nicole and Elaine did not exhibit the third level of reflection in their video annotations. However, it may be assumed that Nicole and Elaine had the potential to move to the third level if guidance and probing questions were provided. Typically, educators would not think to reflect on the moral, ethical, and social issues of education without guidance because they are, most likely, only reflecting on student behavior and teaching skills and strategies.

In Elaine's case study, she wrote in one video annotation:

> Manny struggled to read sight words as well as many other cvc and cvce words that were in his text. He also had a difficult time staying focused while conversations with the two other students were going on, regarding their texts.

With guidance and the use of probing questions, this Level-1 reflection can be transformed to a Level-3 reflection. Elaine identified two problems: struggling to read cvc and cvce words and difficulty staying focused, but she never identified a solution.

Simple probing questions could move this Level-1 reflection to a strong Level-2 reflection, questions such as: What could you do differently in the next lesson to ensure more success in reading cvc and cvce words and to help Manny stay focused? What different approach could you take in teaching cvc and cvce words?

But moving Elaine's reflection to a Level 3 would require different probing questions, such as: Why do you think Manny was struggling with skills that should have been mastered by this time in second grade? Why do you think Manny may be having difficulty focusing?

A final question could concern educational policy. For instance, Elaine could be asked to reflect on how Manny's reading abilities, which were below grade level, impact his progression in the Common Core State Standards and what actions should be taken to help him. For example, should instruction focus solely on skills, and if so, how would this impact the higher-level critical thinking skills outlined in the Common Core Standards?

These probing questions would allow Elaine to reflect on educational policy and the moral and ethical implications of her instruction, thus moving her reflection to van Manen's (1977) critical reflection stage. Further questions to guide teachers through the three levels of reflections can be found in a subsequent section of this book.

BARRIERS TO REFLECTION

Even though teachers are naturally inclined toward reflection, barriers still exist that inhibit educators from developing their reflection skills to the fullest potential. One barrier is the difficulty inherent in the task of reflection. To some, reflection may even appear threatening because it forces us to be honest with ourselves and recognize not only our successes but also areas in which we need to improve. In other words, it forces us to take responsibility for our teaching and learning.

Essentially, being a reflective practitioner is like being your own observer and critical friend (Scales 2012). Through reflection, it is difficult to admit that you do not know everything or that what you are doing may not be effective. The modifying factor is that these weaknesses were identified in reflection and then acted on to better meet the needs of the students.

Jaeger (2013) identifies other barriers to reflection. One such barrier is that educators lack the skills needed to be an effective reflector, such as having a deficit in analytical skills. Analytical skills are important because they allow educators to think deeply about the occurrences in their classroom, the possibilities behind these occurrences, and the possible solutions. Without analytical thought, reflection would not be effective.

Another barrier is the presence of the educator's personal characteristics. For instance, the educator may have an ego and feel that everything he or she is doing is perfectly correct and does not see the need for reflection to improve practice. Another personal characteristic may be that the educator does not have a growth mind-set.

Limitations of the teaching professional are also a barrier. Teachers in today's schools have heavy day-to-day demands, and there may not be time for deep reflection. Also, in some schools, reflection is not a focus, so teachers may not feel the need to practice.

Finally, the school district structure may hinder reflection. The school district may be using a curriculum that does not focus on reflection, or teachers may not teach their own students to be reflective thinkers. Further, new innovations might not be welcomed, which leads to teachers being unmotivated to research and try new strategies.

Clearly, barriers exist that limit the level of teacher reflection. However, generative type activities can be used that help educators develop their reflection to the fullest potential (Jaeger 2013). These generative activities include, but are not limited to, journal entries, case studies, self-studies, and the analysis of video-recorded lessons.

Teacher reflection is a valuable action that elicits changes in practice and ultimately improves student learning. The use of video is a unique and potentially powerful tool that prompts teacher reflection on a complexity of teaching and learning.

KEY CONTENTS

- Definition of reflection
- Three levels of teacher reflection
- Video-based reflection
- Barriers to reflection

REFERENCES

Baecher, L. H., and Tuten, J. (2011). Directed peer response in differentiated approaches to the video analysis of teaching. *Excelsior: Leadership in Teaching and Learning, 5*(2), 30–43.

Christ, T., Arya, P., and Chiu, M. M. (2012). Collaborative peer video analysis: Insights about literacy assessment and instruction. *Journal of Literacy Research, 44*(2), 171–99.

Corcoran, C. A., and Leahy, R. (2003). Growing professionally through reflective practice. *Kappa Delta Pi Record, 40*(1), 30–33.

Danielson, C. (2013). *Framework for teaching evaluation instrument.* Retrieved November 10, 2018, from www.danielsongroup.org.

Dewey, J. (1933). How we think: A restatement of the relation of reflective thinking to the educative process. Boston, MA: Houghton Mifflin.

Hatton, N., and Smith, D. (1995). Reflection in teacher education: Towards definition and implementation. *Teaching and Teacher Education, 11*(1), 33–49.

Jaeger, E. L. (2013). Teacher reflection: Supports, barriers, and results. *Issues in Teacher Education, 22*(1), 89–104.

Kleinknecht, M., and Schneider, J. (2013). What do teachers think and how do they feel when they analyze videos of themselves teaching and of other teacher teaching? *Teaching and Teacher Education, 33*, 13–23. dx.doi.org/10.1016/j.tate.2013.02.00.

Marsh, B., Mitchell, N., and Adamczyk, P. (2010). Interactive video technology: Enhancing professional learning in initial teacher education. *Computers and Education, 54*(3), 742–48.

Nagro, S. A., and Cornelius, K. E. (2013). Evaluating the evidence base of video analysis: A special education teacher development tool. *Teacher Education and Special Education, 36*(4), 312–29.

Rich, P. J., and Tripp, T. (2011). Ten essential questions educators should ask when using video annotation tools. *TechTrends, 55*(6), 16–24.

Rosaen, C. L., Carlisle, J. F., Mihocko, E., Melnick, A., and Johnson, J. (2013). Teachers learning from analysis of other teachers' reading lessons. *Teaching and Teacher Education, 35*, 170–84.

Scales, P. (2012). *Teaching in the lifelong learning sector,* 2nd ed. London, UK: Open University Press.

Schon, D. (1983) *The reflective practitioner.* London, UK: Temple Smith.

Seidel, T., Stürmer, K., Blomberg, G., Kobarg, M., and Schwindt, K. (2011). Teacher learning from analysis of videotaped classroom situations: Does it make a difference whether teachers observe their own teaching or that of others? *Teaching and Teacher Education, 27*, 259–67.

Shanahan, L. E., and Tochelli, A. L. (2014). Examining the use of video study groups for developing literacy pedagogical content knowledge of critical elements of strategy instruction with elementary teachers. *Literacy Research and Instruction, 53*, 1–24.

Sparks-Langer, G. M., and Colton, A. M. (1991). Synthesis of research on teachers' reflective thinking. *Educational Leadership, 48*(6), 37–44.

Sterrett, W., Dikkers, A. G., and Parker, M. (2014). Using brief instructional video clips to foster communication, reflection, and collaboration in schools. *The Educational Forum, 78*, 263–74.

Tripp, T. R., and Rich, P. J. (2012). The influence of video analysis on the process of teacher change. *Teaching and Teacher Education, 28*, 728–39.

van Es, E. A. (2010). A framework for facilitating productive discussions in video club. *Educational Technology, 50*(1), 8–12.

van Es, E. A. (2012). Examining the development of a teacher learning community: The case of a video club. *Teaching and Teacher Education, 28*, 182–92.

van Es, E. A., and Sherin, M. G. (2010). The influence of video clubs on teachers' thinking and practice. *Journal of Math Teacher Education, 13*, 155–76.

van Manen, M. (1977). Linking ways of knowing with ways of being practical. *Curriculum Inquiry, 6*(3), 205–28.

van Manen, M. (1991). Reflectivity and the pedagogical moment: The normativity of pedagogical thinking and acting. *The Journal of Curriculum Studies, 23*(6), 507–36.

van Manen, M. (1995). On the epistemology of reflective practice. *Teachers and Teaching: Theory and Practice, 1*(1), 33–50.

Zhang, M., Lundeberg, M. A., Koehler, M. J., and Eberhardt, J. (2011). Understanding affordances and challenges of three types of video for teacher professional development. *Teaching and Teacher Education, 27*(2), 454–62.

Zeichner, K. (2008). A critical reflection as a goal for teacher education. *Education and Society, 29*(103), 535–54.

Zeichner, K., and Liston, D. (1987). Teaching student teachers to reflect. *Harvard Educational Review, 37*(1), 23–49.

Chapter 4

Deepening Teacher Learning with Video Clubs

Carrie E. Hong and Irene Van Riper

Advances in digital videography have led to an increased use of video in teacher education. Videos provide easier access to observe authentic teaching. Video recording of classroom events can trigger collaborative discussions among members of professional-learning communities. It is considered one of the most powerful learning tools for stimulating teacher learning and growth.

This chapter reviews video clubs as an educational tool to promote collaborative learning among teachers. Teacher video clubs can provide opportunities for professional development for teachers to practice their analytic and leadership skills. Based on a pilot study that investigated teachers' engagement in video clubs, this chapter highlights the potential of teacher video clubs to be an exemplar of video-based learning communities.

The pilot study presents a case of the professional video clubs run by in-service teachers who were enrolled in a graduate program for teacher education. Through a literacy curricular course, teachers engaged in a series of video analyses and exercised their professional skills by leading a video club with their peers. The study examines how teachers participated in video clubs and exchanged ideas to reflect on best practices.

Specifically, the study focuses on teachers' engagement with video analysis in which they practice noticing, interpreting, and analyzing specific features of classroom interactions. Benefits and challenges of video clubs as a professional learning tool are also explored.

A video analysis protocol, presented in this chapter, will model how to effectively engage teachers in video-based professional development.

VIDEO ANALYSIS IN ADVANCING PEDAGOGY

The landscape of teacher education is rooted in reflection and analysis. If teachers are required to grow, they must have some consistent means by which to view and measure their pedagogical development. Wright (2008) explains that when teachers implement a guided video analysis, there is positive impact on their use of reflection. This, in turn, strengthens pedagogy.

The need for guided analytical reflection of instructional pedagogy is facilitated by the use of short video clips of the classroom environment (Nind, Kilburn, and Wiles 2015). Data gleaned from this type of reflective practice fosters a variety of modes in which teachers are able to capture their methods of teaching.

Tripp and Rich (2012a) report that when teachers are analyzing the video recordings taken from their classroom practice, it should begin with active reflection. They define reflection "as a self-critical, investigative process wherein teachers consider the effect of their pedagogical decisions on their situated practice with the aim of improving those practices" (Tripp and Rich 2012a, 678).

When teachers view their pedagogy in the broad strokes of the classroom environment, they are inclined to reflect on the strategies that worked well and, conversely, the ones that did not work successfully in their classroom.

The research is rich with strong evidence for the implementation of video analysis to strengthen pedagogy. Its use is effective for pre-service teachers in their practicum, novice teachers just embarking on their careers, and in-service teachers who wish to ensure success for all of their students. Video analysis and reflection is a flexible tool that can be adapted and modified for all levels of educators in programs for teacher preparation and in classrooms from grades preK to 12 (Cahalan 2013; Wetzel, Maloch, and Hoffman 2016).

Video-based reflection works especially well in strengthening practicum experiences for pre-service teachers. Often, when teacher candidates step into the classroom, they are ill prepared to cope with the multitasking that is required of them. Cahalan (2013) offers strategies to help teacher candidates analyze their video recording and improve their practicum experiences.

Wetzel, Maloch, and Hoffman (2016) allude to a model called CARE in use with pre-service teacher candidates. This model emphasizes collaboration, content-focused coaching, appreciative stances, reflection, and experiential aspects of a continuity of conversations. With the underpinnings of strong coaching, this study frames video-based analysis with practice and rich discussions.

Likewise, Baecher and Connor (2010) describe an initiative called the Video Analysis of Teaching (VAT) as a source for archived videos available to instructors and teacher candidates. Pre-service teachers contribute to this collection and are also able to study other videos to discuss and reflect on what was observed in the video clip.

An assignment for viewing the videos is aligned with the practicum. Teacher candidates must watch the clip three times with a specific purpose in mind for each viewing. This outline structures analysis of the clips and leads to discussion and feedback. The outcomes of this program are effective and lay the foundation for collaborative and ongoing discourse related to special education pedagogy.

Furthermore, Sherin and Linsenmeier (2011) highlight the use and effectiveness of video clubs. Teachers who are engaged in video clubs can develop the skills to target specific interactions and details that occur in their classroom. Through a professional community of peers, discussion becomes the path for analysis of video clips that present the details of student understanding. Sherin and Linsenmeier (2011) offer examples of constructive conversation to inform teachers' instruction.

During a lesson, a teacher may not notice the student who is struggling, who is confused, or too shy to ask questions. Video-based reflection, in conjunction with worthwhile discussions, is a useful tool to unearth any problems that might not be seen by the teacher who is looking with a broader view of the entire classroom.

Research shows that video analysis helps teachers and teacher candidates notice the most essential aspects of their instruction when given the structure to identify these components (Amador and Weiland 2015). Many studies underscore the need for guided analysis, helping novice teachers develop a frame of reference in analyzing classroom interactions (Cahalan 2013; Hong and Van Riper 2016; Wetzel, Maloch, and Hoffman 2016).

It is important that new teachers capture the same level of noticing as more experienced teachers. Thus, video-based reflections are a trajectory for deep conversations that are analytical and foster a high level of awareness for situated practice.

PROFESSIONAL ABILITIES OF VIDEO ANALYSIS

Video-based reflection has been used in the education of teachers for many decades (Gaudin and Charliès 2015). Research has examined ways teachers refine their instructional practices to enhance student learning. Recordings of authentic classroom lessons serve as a unique and powerful medium in which to discuss and improve teacher practices.

Nevertheless, video analysis is not a routine practice that most teachers are trained to do. To maximize the benefits of video as a tool for professional development, recent research proposes the development of an observation framework that can be used in programs for teacher education and professional development (Hollingsworth and Clarke 2017; Rosaen, Carlisle, Mihocko, Melnick, and Johnson 2013; van Es, Tunney, Goldsmith, and Seago 2014).

For instance, Hollingsworth and Clarke (2017) proposed an observation framework to observe, analyze, and discuss practice. The framework includes five dimensions of instructional practice, and each dimension has several elements on which teachers would focus.

Teachers in the pilot study reported that the observation framework helped them reflect on specific areas of instructional practice that they needed to improve. The teachers also valued the analytic process of video-based reflection for their professional growth.

Research shows that teacher abilities are developmental as their knowledge and skills continue to grow over time with practice and experience (see Christ, Arya, and Chiu 2014; Hong and Van Riper 2016; Kavanagh and Rainey 2017; Nagro and Cornelius 2013). For example, novice teachers start to notice and identify what has been observed in the video.

Novice teachers start to differentiate among classroom events and behaviors. Then, with increased experience and professional development, teachers are able to reflect on what has been observed in a context of lesson objectives and outcomes of student learning.

Furthermore, experienced teachers with training in video analysis are able to link classroom events to their conceptual understanding of teaching and learning or to connect theory and practice. The growth model of professional abilities from novice to experienced teachers has implications in understanding how teachers perceive and engage through video-based activities for professional learning.

Based on Blomberg, Sherin, Renkl, Glogger, and Seidel (2014), three levels of professional abilities are observed when teachers engage in video-based reflection: description, evaluation, and integration. A definition of each level follows.

1. Description: one is able to identify what has been observed or to differentiate among classroom events and behaviors.
2. Evaluation: one is able to reflect on what has been observed in a context of lesson objectives and outcomes of student learning.
3. Integration: one is able to link classroom events to her or his conceptual understanding of teaching and learning or to connect theory and practice.

The development of teachers' ability from description, evaluation, and to integration demonstrates a continuum of teacher experience and practice. More specifically, experienced teachers are likely to be competent in describing classroom events with justification for why things are that way.

The difference between novice and experienced teachers relates to how they connect theory and practice in an explicit way. Novice teachers need guided practice in the evaluation of best practices. Training and practice may be required for novice teachers to fully integrate their pedagogical knowledge into instructional practice.

Research reports that teachers demonstrated varied competencies when they engaged in video-based professional development (Maclean and White 2007). They attributed the differences to the availability of teacher training in video analysis. Research recommends that video-based reflection be implemented earlier in programs of teacher education so that it plays a significant role in the development of teachers' professional abilities (Brunvand 2010; Tripp and Rich 2012a).

THE STUDY

The purpose of this pilot study was to examine teachers' professional abilities to notice, interpret, and analyze specific features of classroom interactions. The study also investigated benefits and challenges of teacher video clubs as a tool for professional learning. The study used narrative and descriptive approaches to analyze data sources.

Qualitative methods were selected to generate hypotheses based on themes that naturally emerged from the data (Merriam 1998). Qualitative procedures were used to examine ways in which the study participants engaged in video-club discussions. Analysis of multiple sources of data was completed using constant comparison methods (Glaser and Strauss 1967).

The study was done in a graduate literacy course that focused on adolescent and adult literacy. The course was taught completely online using an online-learning platform and course-management system.

The first author of this chapter (CEH) was the course instructor. Participants were twenty-one graduate students. Seventeen of them were practicing teachers placed in general or special-education settings. Four of them were school librarians. The participants taught in a wide range of grades, pre–K to college. As a note, any names used in this chapter are pseudonyms.

Data sources are the instructor's observations of video analysis practices, video-club discussions, and responses from the survey after the course. Participants' online postings to the discussion forums were observed and analyzed. Written interactions between participants and leaders of the video club were analyzed to find recurrent patterns.

A voluntary and anonymous online survey was distributed at the end of the course. Participants' survey responses were compiled to document their background information and reactions to video clubs. The study was also interested in participants' leadership skills in facilitating collaborative learning with peers.

Practice in Video Analysis

Before leading a video club, a set of practice sessions was provided through the course's discussion forums. The course instructor set up the practice sessions to orient participants regarding how to analyze videos of other teachers and use them for collaborative discussions. Teachers participated in a total of four sessions of video analysis before they started their own video club.

Each practice session focused on different aspects of literacy instruction, such as:

a. lesson purpose and design,
b. instruction,
c. student engagement and participation, and
d. assessment.

These four domains of instruction were selected because they represent important aspects of classroom lessons. Participants were informed that features of the video might relate to more than one domain, and they were encouraged to discuss all relevant domains and aspects of lessons.

During the practice sessions, the instructor modeled and scaffolded strategies for participants, so they had ample opportunities to practice noticing, interpreting, and analyzing specific features of classroom videos. Using an open discussion, participants were able to see each other's posts and have a collaborative discussion as a group.

The instructor carefully selected each video to ensure that the video presented a snapshot of classroom instruction and student interactions. Video clips were selected from various educational sources. A link to the video was provided at the beginning of the online post. The length of each clip was no more than six minutes. An example protocol of sessions for video analysis follows:

> The video introduces how Ms. Vega uses an instructional strategy called "Learning Menus" to provide differentiated support for her seventh-grade students in US History class. Think of the following questions while watching the video and share your thoughts in response to the prompt below.
>
> Questions to consider in terms of lesson purpose and design:

1. Did the teacher help students understand what they would be learning and why?
2. Did the lesson provide students with opportunities to apply what they learned in reading and/or writing?
3. What is the rationale of using "Learning Menus" for differentiated instruction?
4. If you were Ms. Vega, how would you justify the design of this lesson?

Prompt: with the purpose and design of the lesson in mind, please comment on a few effective features of the lesson.

Enthusiasm: Some participants were more active in posting a lengthy response than others. If a video sparked their interest, more frequent interactions in a discussion forum were observed. Because each practice session addressed different domains of classroom instruction, participants tried to focus their attention on a specific domain and exchanged their ideas about it. One participant, Nicole, posted the following:

I enjoyed watching this video and learned a great deal on the learning menu idea since I have never heard of it before. I love the way the whole class was involved in a differentiated activity. I also like that the teacher gave a quick formative assessment of the part the individual students were on before they were able to move the next course. I found the way she scaffolded the activities, from the appetizer being one type of learning, to the main course where the students dug deeper with their thinking an effective strategy. An idea such as this allows for all students to be engaged and held accountable for the work. We often do choice boards in my classroom, where the students are to choose 3 activities in a tic-tac-toe style for differentiation and engagement. I like the idea of a learning menu and will incorporate this when we begin our next classroom novel next week.

In this post, Nicole presented her analysis of the learning menu idea as a strategy to provide differentiated learning opportunities for students. She also made connections to her own teaching by stating that her students engaged in similar activities for the purpose of differentiation and engagement.

Leading a Video Club

The purpose of practicing video analysis was for all participants to become familiar with it. Then individual participants were asked to run a video club of their own as a leader. The following step-by-step directions were provided:

1. Select a video that you feel confident analyzing in depth.
2. Identify domains (e.g., lesson design/purpose, teacher instruction, student engagement, assessment, or any other topics you would like to add, such as diversity, equity, collaboration, etc.) for viewers to pay attention to.

3. Choose questions and prompts from the suggested list and modify them to fit in the selected video. Be specific about what kinds of questions viewers need to answer while watching the video, so the discussion can be focused and thorough.
4. Assist viewers in analyzing the video from a critical viewpoint. Video analysis is not to determine best or mediocre practices. Watching another teacher's video is an opportunity to reflect on one's own instructional practice.

A suggested list of questions and prompts for each domain was provided. Questions and prompts were adapted from Rosaen et al. (2013). As needed, participants received assistance by the course instructor in such areas as selection of an appropriate video clip, polishing questions and prompts, and posting a video.

All participants selected a wide range of videos with various topics and grade levels. Some participants contacted the instructor to consult regarding their video selection. A few participants sought assistance in polishing their questions and prompts. An example posted by one of the participants, Jessica, follows. She was a fourth-grade teacher in a suburban school.

> Subject: "Passing Notes" to Exchange Idea
> [A video link was provided.]
> In this video, Ms. Brown has her sixth-grade language arts students collaboratively analyze text using her "Passing Notes" activity. This strategy requires students to respond to a quote or prompt about the text, Seed Folks, by Paul Fleischman. Students must then trade responses, or "notes," with their classmates and respond to their peer's thoughts. Use evidence from the video and the attached lesson plan to support your answer.
> 1. Did features of the lesson engage the students' interest and participation? Use evidence from the attached transcript to support your response.
> 2. Was there sufficient opportunity for the students to discuss texts and/or contribute to reflections on literacy concepts and processes?
>
> Prompt: With students' engagement and participation in mind, please comment on a few effective features of the lesson.

After posting her initial message, Jessica monitored the online discussion forum and facilitated discussions with her peers for a week. Her peers responded to Jessica's prompt from multiple perspectives. For example, an elementary teacher, Shauna, responded to Jessica's prompt on student engagement and participation as follows:

> Thank you for sharing this video! I really enjoyed watching it, and can see why any student would get excited to "pass notes" in class. I think this is a really

engaging way to give students a chance to respond to a text they are reading. Knowing one of their peers will read their response creates for more of an exciting way to write their response. In my experience, I know some students can get lazy when responding to a text if no one new (other than the teacher) reads their response. This assignment will make students more conscious of what they are writing, knowing multiple classmates will be reading it. This would also be a great opportunity to have the struggling writers read comments written by some of the higher writers.

Ms. Brown had mentioned she often lets the original writer give a final comment in their note. I thought this would be an excellent way to make sure students are understanding the assignment and interpreting their peers' comments correctly. The "Passing Notes" assignment also led to an engaging conversation by the end of the video. Students were able to share comments that stood out to them. I would think this would be a great conversation starter for students who are often too shy to share their ideas. I thought this lesson showed an original and creative take on getting students to respond to a text in a meaningful way. This is definitely a lesson I will keep in mind to use in my own classroom!

As a leader, Jessica closely monitored her club members' posts in response to her initial post. She appreciated her peers' observations and these issues that were raised. Jessica's follow-up response to Shauna's post was as follows:

Thanks for your response! You pointed out two great scaffolding opportunities that I had not noticed! By looking at their peer's responses, students would certainly have the opportunity to learn from each other's thinking and raise the level of their own responses. Knowing that other students will be reading their ideas is also motivating for reluctant readers and/or writers, as they would probably want to impress their peers.

The other scaffold you highlighted was the closing conversation. Because students had the chance to read several students' ideas and think of their own responses during the activity, they are more prepared to share at the end. This would certainly make it easier for shy or struggling students to participate in the discussion, which they might not always have the chance to do. I am glad you liked the strategy and hope you get the chance to try it in your own classroom!

In this response post, Jessica demonstrated her leadership skills by highlighting instructional strategies observed in the video. As a leader, she attempted to analyze peer responses and use them for others to learn from.

For example, Jessica started her post by restating Shauna's post, stating: "You pointed out two great scaffolding opportunities that I had not noticed!" Then, she evaluated Shauna's observations in a constructive manner.

TEACHERS' VARIED ABILITIES IN VIDEO ANALYSIS

The study shows that video analysis benefited teachers because they had opportunities to observe a variety of instructional strategies and to apply their analytic and leadership skills from participating in video clubs. Survey responses reflect how the study participants perceive and approach video analysis as a learning tool and what they think of video clubs as an opportunity for professional development in school settings.

Experience in Video Analysis

A voluntary and anonymous survey was implemented. Thirteen out of twenty-one participants (62 percent) completed the survey (see appendix A). A mixed group of beginning and experienced educators responded to the survey questions: Seven participants with more than ten years of experience, three participants with five to ten years of teaching experience, and three participants with two to four years of teaching experience.

When asked a question of their experience in a video club, ten participants (77 percent) responded that it was their first time leading and participating in video clubs. Three participants (23 percent) responded that they had prior experience with video clubs. They were asked if they would like to try a video club with colleagues in their school. Seven participants (54 percent) responded that they would like to try a video club with their colleagues. Five participants (35 percent) responded that they were not sure.

When running a video club with peers, participants applied their analytic and leadership skills. Each participant selected a video clip with questions and prompts to lead a productive discussion. Selection of videos reflects, to some extent, their interests and teaching.

For example, teachers in special-education settings selected a video clip that featured differentiated instruction for diverse learners. Teachers who taught at middle grades selected a video clip that represented social and collaborative learning among students.

Teacher Buy-Ins

When it comes to their competency of initialing a video club as a tool for professional learning, participant responses varied. Eight participants (61.4 percent) responded that they felt comfortable to some extent, from slightly to extremely, about initiating a video club in their school. Three participants (23 percent) responded they felt uncomfortable about initiating a video club in their school.

In responding to open-ended questions, participants stated their reaction to the video club activities. A few teachers reported they struggled to find appropriate videos that lead to successful discussions. For example, one participant wrote: "Only challenge was finding one that was an appropriate length to view and not lose interest."

Additionally, some reported that selecting questions and prompts was also a challenge. One participant wrote: "I only realized that after I posted my video and facilitated discussions I was able to think of deeper questions to ask."

Positive Learning Experience

A majority of the participants reported video clubs provided them with a meaningful learning experience. One teacher wrote: "I enjoyed leading a video club as it let me exchange information with professional teachers and taught me many different ways to look at an issue." Another response addressed the value of teacher video clubs for continued growth:

> I have learned that there truly are endless opportunities to share knowledge and video clubs make it that much easier to continue to be lifelong learners!

Participants also highlighted the collaborative opportunities that video clubs offer. They liked to work with colleagues and share ideas from multiple perspectives. One participant described the value of video analysis in expanding the scope of their professionalism:

> I really liked the activity. It's interesting to hear other people's perspectives around the same lesson. I also liked the variety of topics that I was able to learn about. For example, I have no experience working with English Language Learners (ELLs), so I found those videos really interesting and learned something I would not have typically.

Participants appreciated the opportunity to analyze the video from multiple perspectives. They regarded it as a means of sharing ideas and learn new strategies collaboratively. Participants with previous experience with video analysis attempted to integrate their pedagogical knowledge and skills in responding to peers during the discussions of the video club. One participant described the value of video discussions like this:

> I liked how everyone shared something that they enjoyed and that had some type of connection to them and even more so, when classmates shared something that they didn't know much about and they wanted to dive deeper with us, as their discussion grew.

BENEFITS AND CHALLENGES OF VIDEO CLUBS

Increased engagement and collaboration were observed when participants took part in video analysis and video clubs. Teachers exchanged their ideas and had common ground on which to relate the video they watched to issues relevant to their own teaching. Once a mutual understanding of teaching contexts was established, teachers shared their analytic viewpoints on a given topic and probed even deeper and wider.

In survey responses after the course, participants mentioned the benefits of video clubs for their own learning. Specifically, two participants stated they were visual learners and benefited from watching videos to enhance their learning, and 92 percent of the participants mentioned positive outcomes from their engagement in the video clubs. For example, one participant valued short videos as a means of reviewing best practices by stating:

> I love how informative short videos can be for instruction. I am not in a classroom but have shared many of the ideas that I have been exposed to as a result of this experience. This is a great way to be exposed to exemplary teaching without having to take a whole day away from the actual job.

Teachers had opportunities to watch videos that featured various instructional strategies and classroom issues. Respondents mentioned that watching a variety of classroom videos increased their competency in specific issues such as differentiation, student engagement, co-teaching, and instruction for students with special needs.

Some visual learners said they benefited from using visual resources to improve their learning. The value of digital videography was also recognized by teachers. One teacher responded that he or she would like to expand the use of video resources in classroom lessons to improve student learning.

Despite the benefits addressed by participants of the study, challenges were also noticed. The survey results revealed teachers' varied experience with video analysis. Technical familiarity with video technology and online learning may have influenced the outcomes of video clubs offered in an online graduate course. It is recommended that a sufficient amount of time for teachers to practice video analysis is needed to take full advantage of video-based professional development.

Similarly, it was observed that teachers' readiness to engage in video analysis varied. Teachers approach video-based professional learning in different ways because participants have a wide range of prior experience and training in video analysis. One's attitude toward video as a technology tool may influence the way participants engage in video-based reflection. As video analysis was not a mandatory component of their professional qualifications, one may assume that teachers perceive the practice of video analysis on an individual basis.

The study has its limitations. It did not examine teachers' readiness to implement a video club in their own school, other than self-reporting. Additional and ongoing professional development will benefit teachers in improving their analytic and leadership skills for video-based professional learning.

Furthermore, the study did not include teachers' abilities to analyze their own videos. Future research may examine the potential of video-based evaluation to assess teacher qualifications (Kersting, Givvin, Thompson, Santagata, and Stigler 2012). Further investigation is needed to examine video clubs in which teachers use their own videos and lead a discussion in a video club with their peers.

KEY CONTENTS

- Professional abilities of video analysis
- Pilot study on teacher video clubs
- Benefits and challenges of video clubs

REFERENCES

Amador, J., and Weiland, I. (2015). What preservice teachers and knowledgeable others professionally notice during lesson study. *The Teacher Educator, 50*, 109–26.

Baecher, L. H., and Connor, D. J. (2010). "What do you see?' Using video analysis of classroom practice in a preparation program for teachers of students with learning disabilities. *Insights on learning Disabilities, 7*(2), 5–18.

Blomberg, G., Sherin, M. G., Renkl, A., Glogger, I., and Seidel, T. (2014). Understanding video as a tool for teacher education: Investigating instructional strategies integrating video to promote reflection. *Instructional Science, 42*(3), 443–63. Doi: 10.1007/s11251-013-9281-6.

Brunvand, S. (2010). Best practices for producing video content for teacher education. *Contemporary Issues in Technology and Teacher Education, 10*(2), 247–56.

Christ, T., Arya, P., and Chiu, M. M. (2014). Teachers' reports of learning and application to pedagogy based on engagement in collaborative peer video analysis. *Teaching Education, 25*(4), 349–74.

Cahalan, J. M. (2013). Teaching classroom videorecording analysis to graduate students: Strategies for observation and improvement. *College Teaching, 61*, 44–50.

Gaudin, G., and Charliès, S. (2015). Video viewing in teacher education and professional development: A literature review. *Educational Research Review, 16*, 41–67.

Glaser, B. G., and Strauss, A. L. (1967). *The discovery of grounded theory: Strategies for qualitative research*. Chicago, IL: Aldine.

Hollingsworth, H., and Clarke, D. (2017). Video as a tool for focusing teacher self-reflection: Supporting and provoking teacher learning. *Journal of Mathematics Teacher Education, 20*(5), 457–75.

Hong, C. E., and Van Riper, I. (2016). Enhancing teacher learning from guided video analysis of literacy instruction: An interdisciplinary and collaborative approach. *Journal of Inquiry and Action in Education, 7*(2), 94–110.

Kavanagh, S. S., and Rainey, E. C. (2017). Learning to support adolescent literacy: Teacher educator pedagogy and novice teacher take up in secondary English language arts teacher preparation. *American Educational Research Journal, 54*(5), 904–37.

Kersting, N. B., Givvin, K. B., Thompson, B. J., Santagata, R., and Stigler, J. W. (2012). Measuring usable knowledge: Teachers' analyses of mathematics classroom videos predict teaching quality and student learning. *American Educational Research Journal, 49*(3), 568–89.

Maclean, R., and White, S. (2007). Video reflection and the formation of teacher identity in a team of pre-service and experienced teachers. *Reflective Practice: International and Multidisciplinary Perspectives, 8*(1), 47–60. doi:10.1080/14623940601138949.

Merriam, S. B. (1998). *Qualitative research and case study applications in education.* San Francisco, CA: Jossey-Bass Publishers.

Nagro, S. A., and Cornelius, K. E. (2013). Evaluating the evidence base of video analysis: A special education teacher development tool. *Teacher Education and Special Education, 36*(4), 312–29.

Nind, M., Kilburn, D., and Wiles, R. (2015). Using video and dialogue to generate pedagogic knowledge: Teachers, learners and researchers reflecting together on the pedagogy of social research methods. *International Journal of Social Research Methodology, 18*(5), 561–76.

Rosaen, C. L., Carlisle, J. F., Mihocko, E., Melnick, A., and Johnson, J. (2013). Teachers learning from analysis of other teachers' reading lessons. *Teaching and Teacher Education, 35*, 170–84.

Sherin, M. G., and Linsenmeier, K. A. (2011). Pause, rewind, reflect: Video clubs open the classroom doors. *Journal of Staff Development, 32*(5), 38–41.

Tripp, T. R., and Rich, P. J. (2012a). The influence of video analysis on the process of teacher change. *Teaching and Teacher Education, 28*, 728–39.

Tripp, T. R., and Rich, P. J. (2012b). Using video to analyze one's own teaching. *British Journal of Educational Technology, 43*(4), 678–704.

van Es, E. A., Tunney, J., Goldsmith, L. T., and Seago, N. (2014). A framework for the facilitation of teachers' analysis of video. *Journal of Teacher Education, 65*(4), 340–56.

Wetzel, M. M., Maloch, B., and Hoffman, J. V. (2016). Retrospective video analysis: A reflective tool for teachers and teacher educators. *The Reading Teacher, 70*(5), 533–42.

Wright, G. A. (2008). *Improving teacher performance using an enhanced digital video reflection technique.* IADIS International Conference on Cognition and Exploratory Learning in Digital Age, Freiburg, Germany, 381–84.

Chapter 5

Online Video Sharing for Teacher Assessment

Alex Chambers

Assessment of in-service teachers is necessary if there is to be any growth and progress in the quality of teaching and learning in the classroom. Sound and structured assessment can provide teachers a fresh perspective and useful feedback—things that they themselves likely cannot take note of while they are in the process of teaching.

However, conducting assessment and providing feedback can be quite a time-consuming endeavor. Having limited time and scheduling conflicts can make this even more difficult. With an obvious need for assessment, and the reality of a limited amount of time during the school day, one solution is to use a streaming video platform such as a video-sharing website to conduct assessment and provide feedback.

STREAMING VIDEO

Streaming video is one of the fastest growing and most popular ways for people to consume a variety of video content. With high-speed Internet increasing in efficiency and becoming more available to the public, many people have now become used to choosing when to view their content, as opposed to waiting for it to be released. Streaming video avoids the need for other types of media, such as a DVD.

Streaming video also allows consumers to view content on a variety of devices, such as smartphones, tablets, laptop and desktop computers, and even on televisions. In addition, many streaming video platforms that are established on video-sharing websites offer not only the ability to view streaming video, but also to provide feedback on that video in the form of comments.

Using a streaming-video platform via a video-sharing website is an efficient, constructive, and time-saving way to provide feedback for in-service teachers. Using this type of website, video can be viewed on demand, and feedback can be shared with the teacher being assessed. In addition, viewing of the video can be limited to only the teacher and assessor. And if desired, other parties can be allowed to access the video.

Lastly, feedback can be delivered one way (e.g., from the assessor to the teacher) or a dialogue can be created between the teacher and the assessor as well as any other party that is allowed video viewing access. This chapter will discuss the research, technical requirements, strategies, and best practices for using a video-streaming platform via a video-sharing website for providing feedback to in-service teachers.

Research on Streaming Video and Teacher Assessment

Video recording to assess teacher effectiveness and student engagement is commonplace across the pre-service and in-service teacher experience. When pre-service teachers enter the classroom for the first time, it is likely they will be required to video record a sample of their teaching to be submitted to their program for assessment.

Should that same teacher wish to advance their teaching credentials and apply for national board certification, they will once again be expected to videotape themselves teaching. In this day and age, it is likely that teachers entering the profession will have some amount of experience in being video recorded or should anticipate being videotaped sometime during their career.

Research in the area of streaming video being used to provide feedback to teachers is limited and confined to examining only the perspectives of pre-service teachers. However, the results of this research demonstrate that using streaming video for this purpose has great potential, both technically and functionally. Two studies in particular have identified the benefits of using streaming video with regard to convenience, flexibility, and video quality.

Streaming Video: Convenience and Quality

Video recording can have limits, particularly with the format of the video itself. If the video is kept in a static format (e.g., a videotape, SD card, USB drive) only those who have it can view it; this makes accessing the video limited. However, if the video was uploaded to a video-sharing site, multiple users could view the video on the Internet, eliminating the limitations of keeping videos in a static format.

Wu and Kao (2008) administered a study that used streaming videos of thirty-six pre-service teachers to examine the effectiveness of web-based peer assessment. Pre-service teachers in this study were able to view videos of themselves and other pre-service teachers on the Internet, as well as provide commentary to each other.

They learned that the pre-service teachers who took part in their study found streaming video to be useful. In particular, they found that viewing streaming video was more convenient than watching the videos in a static format such as a videotape (Wu and Kao 2008).

In addition, they noted that a large majority of these pre-service teachers found that the quality of the streaming videos was acceptable; 72 percent agreed that the video quality was acceptable, and 92 percent agreed that the audio quality was acceptable (Wu and Kao 2008). Although this study focused on the perspectives of pre-service teachers, it is safe to say that using streaming video to assess in-service teachers would be comparable with regard to convenience and quality.

However, Wu and Kao (2008) also identified some challenges to using streaming video as a tool for assessment. For example, some of the pre-service teachers who participated in the study occasionally contributed to technical issues when video recording other pre-service teachers in the act of teaching.

Wu and Kao (2008) stated that if streaming video is to be used as an assessment tool, it is important that those conducting the video recording are properly trained in how to produce a quality video. If the videos produced are inaudible or difficult to see, it is likely that those who are assessing the video will be limited in how much of the recorded teaching they can actually assess.

In short, if the assessor cannot see or hear what was taped, he or she cannot assess it. As with the implementation of any aspect of technology, it is important to note that technical knowledge of said technology is needed to take full advantage of its capabilities.

Streaming Video: Authentic Assessment

As part of the Lifelong Learning Erasmus Network Programme of the European Union, Weststrate and Janssen (2010) examined the use of streaming video as a tool in a video portfolio of teacher competencies for the Language Network for Quality Assurance (LANQUA) Toolkit. They identified that streaming video was an authentic method of examining teacher competencies.

They also noted that using streaming video to examine teacher competencies had "practical benefits such as accessibility of practices, flexibility in updating information, and incorporating video into multimedia resources" (Weststrate and Janssen 2010, 1). These benefits of using streaming video to examine teacher competencies not only have relevance to providing feedback to teachers, but also indicate a convenient way in which to provide that feedback for all parties involved.

TECHNICAL REQUIREMENTS

To take full advantage of the benefits of streaming video, the original videos that are produced must be of high quality. If the purpose of using videos is to assess teacher knowledge, one must be able to easily examine teacher performance. Therefore, the teacher must be clearly seen *and* heard on the video. The proper resources must be considered, including hardware, software, and the necessary training so that the video can be produced with little challenge.

Hardware Options

When it comes to creating high-quality video, there are many options currently available. The most common method that many schools already use is recording video on a portable device such as a smartphone or tablet. Most smartphones and tablets have the ability to shoot video in a variety of formats from low to high quality.

Even though this allows for choice between formats, the higher the quality format used, the clearer the recording will be and the easier it will be to assess. Therefore, it is recommended that the device used to record the video have the capability to record in what is known as 720p. 720p, also known as HD ready, is a common video resolution that provides high-quality video footage and plays back at a standard high-definition television resolution. This resolution, or any higher resolution (e.g., 1080p), will be acceptable.

This particular format is widely available on many devices, allowing for a greater selection of portable devices from which to choose. In addition to offering 720p, the device should also be able to export the video in a format known as MP4.

MP4, sometimes referred to as MPEG-4, is the most-common video format used for streaming. This means that when the video is uploaded for streaming (as will be discussed later in this chapter), there will be little or no chance of incompatibility issues.

In the event that a smartphone or tablet is not available, the use of a digital video camera is another option. Although digital video cameras can be slightly higher in price than smartphones or tablets, they also offer more specific features for shooting video. Again, it is recommended that the video camera have the ability to shoot video at 720p.

In addition, if using a digital video camera, it is recommended that the camera save video data to an SD card, which is a kind of flash memory card.

This is a common feature among many digital video cameras. This is recommended so that video files can be easily transferred from the camera to a computer.

Once it has been determined which type of device will be used to record the video, there remain several other technological considerations to be made. All of these considerations are vital to ensuring that technical issues can be reduced as much as possible.

Internal Storage

Recording high-quality video requires a great deal of storage space because the average 720p video will take up between 40 and 50 MB of space. The typical internal storage on smartphones and tablets can be anywhere between 32 GB on the low end to 256 GB on the high end. Some smartphones and tablets also have options to add up to 128 GB of memory in the form of a micro SD card, which is a removable flash memory card commonly used for storage and widely available at most electronic retailers.

It is recommended that any device being used have a minimum 3 to 5 GB of available space per video. This is to be sure the device does not run out of internal space while videotaping, rendering it unable to record the remainder of whatever teacher activity was being recorded. This can be checked on the device; because devices may vary, please consult the devices' users guide on how to determine available internal storage space.

Stabilization of the Device

It must be determined how the device will be stabilized to record the video. It is not recommended that the device be handheld while recording because this can result in a shaky picture. There are several types of devices available, including tripods, that are specifically designed to hold portable devices, as well as adapters that fit a standard tripod to accommodate a portable device.

An Internet search using the phrase "tripod stand for smartphone" should yield dozens of results. Be sure to determine the function of the tripod in relation to the surface on which it will stand while recording. Also, be sure to read the description of the tripod device carefully to determine if it will be compatible with the device that has been chosen for video recording.

Camera Selection

It should be noted that most smartphones and tablets have cameras that are both front- (i.e. on the same side as the touch screen) and rear facing (i.e. on the backside of the device). It is recommended that any video recording be done with the rear-facing camera. This is because most rear-facing cameras having the ability to record in 720p. Front-facing cameras tend to have a much lower resolution and thus will produce a lower-quality video.

Audio Quality

It is most important to determine the audio recording capabilities of the device. There is a saying in video production; "Two-thirds of video is audio." In other words, when recording a video, if the audio is of poor quality, it will impact the overall video quality. Similarly, if a teacher is video recorded while providing instruction and the audio is not intelligible, it will severely limit the assessor's ability to provide feedback.

Most portable devices have built in microphones that are only designed to capture audio in short range. It is recommended that when recording with a portable device, the device itself be as close to the teacher as possible. One way to determine what is an acceptable distance is to record a brief video (approximately 30 seconds) with the teacher practicing their lesson as if they were teaching it to the class and in the same room where they will be teaching.

The video should be played back to determine if the audio quality is acceptable. If not, the camera should be repositioned and the process repeated until the audio being recorded is of acceptable clarity.

If after several attempts, the audio is still not acceptable, another option is to use an external microphone, placed closer to the teacher and connected to the portable device, which can then be placed further away. This would also allow some increased flexibility as to where the camera and microphone can be placed.

To locate a microphone that is compatible with your device, simply use the Internet search engine of your choice and enter your devices' brand name with the keywords "external microphone." This should yield several results that will be compatible with your device.

Overall, the goal in selecting the hardware should be to choose the equipment that is most accessible, can record the highest quality (i.e., 720p), and can be easily positioned to capture clear video and audio. Choosing the proper equipment will reduce the possibility of any unforeseen technical issues and result in producing a quality video. The assessor can see and hear the teacher clearly and thus be able to provide the most detailed feedback.

SOFTWARE OPTIONS

When the video recording has been completed, there may be a need to alter the file. In some cases only a portion of the video may be needed for assessment, there may be a need for audio and video adjustments, or it may be necessary to convert the file type. If this is the case, there are programs available for video editing.

Software for Video Editing

Software for video editing allows a user to modify a video file that has been recorded. There are a variety of types of software, from the most basic of applications to the more advanced video production. Windows Movie Maker and iMovie are two programs that are available for free and are used on the two most popular operating systems, Windows and Mac.

For a computer using a Windows operating system, Microsoft provides Windows Movie Maker for free. This program allows the user to trim the length of a video or separate one single video into several parts. It also allows the user to adjust the audio volume of the video, making it louder or softer.

Windows Movie Maker is compatible with a variety of video file types and extensions. If the computer running Windows does not have Windows Movie Maker, it can be easily obtained by visiting the website support.microsoft.com and performing a search for Windows Movie Maker.

For Apple users, iMovie is provided free for all MacIntosh computers using OS 8 or later and Apple mobile devices iOS 7 or later. iMovie has a great number of features, including the ability to enhance the audio of a video clip, edit a video clip into segments, and even change the lighting or picture quality. Like Windows Movie Maker, iMovie is also compatible with a variety types of video files.

Converting File Types

Typically, Apple-branded devices (e.g., iPhone, iPad, and MacIntosh) export video in the file type MOV, which is a file type exclusive to Apple products. Conversely, devices that are not Apple brand can export video in the file type of MP4, WMV (Windows Media Video), and various other types. Although most video-sharing websites are compatible with a broad variety of file types, it may be necessary to convert the video file type of the video created for compatibility reasons.

This is another use for the aforementioned programs for video editing because they have the ability to convert video files from one type to another. Because the process of file conversion varies with each program, consult the program's user guide for further information on how to do this.

Software for Screen Capture

Although the use for video has been established in this chapter as a means to assess the physical act of teaching, there are often other aspects to the teaching process that could also be enhanced by using video. With assessing the act of teaching comes the need to assess the planning aspects of teaching, such as lesson plans. Software for screen capture can assist in this process.

This software for screen capture allows a user to snapshot whatever image they have on their computer monitor. In addition, the image will include the cursor of the mouse, which can be used to point to specific details on screen. This software also captures audio via an external microphone through the computer's built-in microphone or an external device.

Using this type of software, an assessor could create an electronic version of a lesson plan (or other teaching preparation document), provide verbal feedback, and also use the pointer of the mouse to indicate which parts of the plan are being examined. Further details on how this type of video can be used as a streaming video will be discussed later in this chapter.

When analyzing if using a video-sharing website would be optimal, there are two considerations: accessibility and infrastructure. If the videos that are to be posted and streamed need to be easily accessible, video-sharing websites do offer that accessibility.

However, some public institutions use firewalls, which are software for Internet security that restricts the accessibility of certain websites, including video-sharing websites. If this is the case, an institution may encounter accessibility issues if they choose to use a video-sharing website. Fortunately, permissions can be adjusted in most firewalls and allow access to video-sharing websites.

Additionally, the infrastructure, specifically the actual physical technology infrastructure that is available, needs to be examined. Bandwidth, or the ability to send data over a wired or wireless connection, must be sufficiently large enough to stream videos, which is typically 2.5 to 4 Mbps (megabits per second). This can be done by performing an Internet search using the key words "speed test" or by contacting the Internet service provider directly.

The hardware to be used to view the streaming videos (e.g., desktop computer, tablet computer, or mobile device such as a smartphone) must also be assessed to establish streaming capability and compatibility.

Streaming Video on Video-Sharing Websites

Once the video has been recorded and finalized (i.e., modified if needed), the video is ready to be assessed. To do this, the video can be uploaded to a video-sharing website. Video-sharing websites, such as YouTube or Vimeo, are often the most accessible, cost effective, and easiest to use. They are available for free, are designed to be user friendly, and support a variety of options for video sharing.

A video-sharing website is a website that will allow an individual user to host videos, control how that video is viewed, and allow viewers to comment on said videos. These options vary, but typically range from publicly viewable (anyone with an Internet connection can search, view, and comment on the video) to posting the video as "unlisted" (not searchable but anyone with a link can view and comment on the video) and privately viewable (not searchable and only those who are given access can view and comment on the video).

Typically, video-sharing websites are used by individuals, businesses, and entrepreneurs who wish to distribute various kinds of video content such as short films or advertisements. However, video-sharing websites can also be used to privately share and comment on videos between two or more individuals.

Examples of some of the most-popular video-sharing websites are YouTube and Vimeo, which allow users to upload and host videos free of charge. One drawback, however, is that video-sharing websites can also add advertisements to any hosted video. This is the main source of revenue for most video-sharing websites and why they are free to use.

Training

Although video-sharing websites are designed to be user friendly, any faculty or staff that will be using the video-sharing website needs to be familiar with how it functions. Fortunately, many video-sharing websites provide a great deal of support to users in the form of a help center.

Both YouTube and Vimeo offer help centers that contain information on the basic uses of the website, such as how to upload and share videos. These help centers provide the most detailed information, enabling users to take full advantage of what these video-sharing websites have to offer. It is recommended that all those who are unfamiliar with video-sharing websites use the help centers to gain familiarity with the main functions of the website.

Accounts

Finally, when using a video-sharing website, anyone who will be uploading, sharing, viewing, and commenting on videos needs go to the site and establish an account. It is recommended that faculty and staff who will be using the video-sharing website use an e-mail address that was assigned by their institution; this way, accounts stay anchored to the institution where the videos and feedback will be used.

Signing up for an account with most video-sharing websites is usually free; however, some offer options of expanded service for a nominal fee. For example, Vimeo offers several account options such as custom video players and higher rates of bandwidth. For most users who will be posting videos to be viewed by three or less people, the free or basic accounts offered tend to suffice.

FEEDBACK OPTIONS

Once a video-sharing website has been chosen, accounts established, equipment acquired, faculty and staff trained or allowed time to become familiar with the video-sharing website, a system of providing feedback can be established. Three main feedback options to be discussed include:

1. providing feedback to in-service teachers based on their daily instruction;
2. monitoring the fidelity of implementation of new instructional materials, such as interventions; and
3. providing feedback on written materials to in-service teachers, such as lesson plans.

The options discussed in this chapter are not by any means an exhaustive list of the possibilities of providing feedback via streaming video. However, these options tend to be the most optimal starting point.

Providing Feedback

In this example, the video-sharing website, YouTube, will be used as the video-sharing website of choice. Teachers first establish how they will be video recording themselves (see previous content) and sign up for an account with YouTube. Once the video has been recorded, they will upload their video to their account.

YouTube offers three settings for uploading a video:

1. public (seen by everyone and is searchable);
2. unlisted (not searchable but viewable by anyone who has the link, and the link can be shared with others); and
3. private (not searchable and only those who receive the link via e-mail will be able to view the video and link is not shareable).

It is recommended that videos be set to either unlisted or private, depending on the level of privacy desired.

Once the video is uploaded, the teacher will share the video with those providing feedback. Feedback can be provided in the comments section, which is typically found below the video. When providing feedback, there are three things to remember. First, to leave a comment, the user must also have an account on the same video-sharing website and be logged in.

Second, when leaving feedback, the user should leave a time stamp as to where in the video the feedback is applicable. A time stamp is the exact time in the video where a specific task or behavior was observed and is directly related to the feedback being provided. This can be found in the lower left-hand corner of the video. Simply pause the video at the time the task or behavior is observed and type the time stamp into the comment section before providing feedback.

Example: "1:14–At this point, you are attending to student responses quite well, which is helping to build rapport with your class."

This way, the teacher will know exactly what to look for and where to go in the video to view the object of the comment. This provides a distinct advantage over discussing an observation made by another person. Discussion relies on teachers having to recall what they may have done, whereas a video clearly provides evidence of exactly what transpired.

Third and most important, criteria for feedback must be mutually established between assessors and those being assessed. This can be done by using criteria from a formal observation or by the person being assessed to inform potential assessors of what they would like feedback on. Although various ways of determining criteria for feedback exist, it is imperative that it be established before video recording.

Also, one must remember that the video can be shared with a variety of people, which allows the teacher to glean feedback from multiple sources and is more challenging to accomplish with in-person observations. For example, the teacher can share the video with other members of their grade-level team to acquire specific feedback on grade-level content.

The teacher could make the video accessible to teachers at different schools to gain insight and ideas on how others are providing instruction regarding the same or similar subjects. In addition, the video could be shared among administrators to gain a deeper understanding of how instruction and learning is occurring in their schools.

Daily Instruction

Although most in-service teachers are observed for annual performance assessments, these in-person assessments tend to happen only once or twice a year. When these observation assessments are later discussed with the teacher, the basic feedback typically comes in the form of what the teacher's strengths are and what areas need improvement. However, there are significant gaps of time in between these observations.

If teachers were to video record their instructional activities and post the video on a video-sharing website, they could solicit formative feedback from administrators or other colleagues. By doing so, they could use this feedback to focus on the areas of improvement that were identified in their formal observation. This could take place without having another person take the time to observe or need to meet with them. Eliminating the potential distraction of an observer in the room is another distinct advantage.

Monitoring Fidelity

When a new curriculum, intervention, or other instructional item is implemented, it is necessary to make sure that it is being used as was intended. This means the monitoring of said instructional item is vital to making sure that not only is it being used properly, but also that students are benefiting from its use.

By video recording and sharing the video, the performance of whoever is delivering the instruction can be assessed and monitored and feedback can be provided to ensure that the instruction is following established protocol. Also, the videos can provide evidence of how the instructional item is being implemented, thus demonstrating efforts and initiatives that are being undertaken to improve student learning.

Written Materials

As discussed previously in this chapter (see "Software for Screen Capture"), there may be a need to provide feedback on written materials, such as lesson plans. By using software to screen capture and create a video, an assessor can provide specific commentary on documents and other materials in electronic form. Most software for screen capturing provides options to annotate a video, and an assessor can identify specific items that need attention.

By creating a video and sharing it via a video-sharing website, whoever the document pertains to can gain insight from the provided feedback without having to schedule a meeting with the person assessing the document. In addition, verbal feedback on a video has the potential to be less subjective. Vocal tone, verbal emphasis, and other characteristics of oral feedback allow for a more robust understanding of feedback as opposed to written feedback.

CONCLUSION

Streaming-video technology has advanced greatly in recent years, and this technology can be used to advantage in assessing the knowledge of, and providing feedback to, in-service teachers. The means with which to record videos can be easily identified because of the abundance of options currently available.

Video-sharing websites provide an easy, accessible, and convenient platform to share videos to be assessed and to provide specific feedback to those who are being assessed. By using video-sharing websites, the assessment of videos can be completed by a wider array of assessors in a shorter amount of time.

Feedback can be based on what is demonstrated in the video and does not rely on the recall abilities of the in-service teacher being assessed. Taking the time to establish and implement a system of using a video-sharing website to assess in-service teacher knowledge and to provide clear and specific feedback can provide a multitude of benefits for all those involved.

KEY CONTENTS

- Streaming video for teaching assessment
- Technical requirements for video recording and sharing
- Video-sharing websites
- Feedback options

REFERENCES

Wu, C. -C., and Kao, H. -C. (2008). Streaming videos in peer assessment to support training pre-service teachers. *Educational Technology and Society*, *11*(1), 45–55.

Weststrate, C., and Janssen, J. (2010). Video portfolio for assessment of teacher competences. *LanQua Toolkit: Example of Practice* (Lifelong Learning Erasmus Network programme of the European Union). Southampton, UK: LanQua, University of Southampton.

Appendix A

Video Analysis Survey

Supplement to Chapter 4

Carrie E. Hong and Irene Van Riper

SURVEY QUESTIONS

1. How many years have you been teaching (preK–adult), excluding student teaching?

    0–1 year.
    2–4 years.
    5–10 years.
    More than 10 years.

2. Prior to taking this course, did you have any experience of engaging in a video club in which teachers watch recordings of classroom lessons and have a discussion around selected topics?

    Yes, I have a video club experience before.
    No, this is my first time participating in video clubs.

3. Would you like to try a video club with colleagues in your school?

    Yes, I would like to.
    I am not sure.
    No, I do not want to.

4. How comfortable do you feel about initiating a video club as a professional learning tool in your school?

    Extremely uncomfortable.
    Moderately uncomfortable.
    Slightly uncomfortable.
    Neither comfortable nor uncomfortable.

Slightly comfortable.
Moderately comfortable.
Extremely comfortable.

5. What do you think of your experience of leading a video club? What have you learned from it?

6. Is there anything you did not like about leading a video club? What challenges did you have (e.g., selecting a video, choosing questions or prompts, promoting a deep analysis of the lesson, facilitating discussions, and so on)?

7. Please share your experience of participating in video clubs of your classmates. What do you like or dislike about it?

Index

audio. *See* microphone
adaptive experts, 16

camera, 60–62
classroom videos, xiii, 6, 13, 20, 48, 54;
    benefit of, 16–18, 30–31;
    types, 6–8
collaboration, ix, xiii, 1–3, 5, 10–11, 14,
    16–18, 20, 22, 31, 43–45, 48–50,
    53–54
Common Core Standards, 38
conceptual framework, xiii, 1

dyslexia, 35

example-rule. *See* rule-example

knowledge based reasoning, 9, 31–32

Language Network for Quality
    Assurance (LANQUA), 59
learning goals (and objectives), 4–6, 8,
    10, 19
learning menus, 48–49

microphone (audio), 62

noticing, 32, 43, 45, 48

observation framework, 46

perceptual process: first level, second
    level, third level, 9
practical action, 28, 37
practice-to-notice, 5
prior knowledge, 2–3, 5, 7
professional development, xiii, 1–2,
    5–11, 16–20, 22, 25, 29–31, 43,
    45–47, 52, 54–55
professional-learning communities, 1,
    11, 17, 30, 43
prompts, 11, 19, 32, 50, 52–53

reflection, x, xiv, 2, 7, 16, 19–20, 22,
    25, 28–29, 31–38, 45;
    barriers to, 39;
    benefits of, 36;
    definition of, 26, 44;
    types of (in action/on action), 26–27;
    van Manen's Stages/Levels, 27–29,
    37;
    video-based, 25, 31, 45–47
retelling, 3
rule-example (example-rule), 20–21

SD card, 58, 60–61
selective attention, 9, 31, 37

software, 1, 30, 60
    file types, 63
    screen capture, 64, 68
stabilization of video. 61
streaming video, xiv, 57–60, 64, 66, 68

video analysis, xiii, 1–11, 16, 19–22, 29–32, 35, 43–50, 52–54
video club analysis models (CARE, VAT), 44
video clubs, xiv, 1, 17–18, 43, 30, 48, 52–55;
    leading on line, 49
video materials, 10
video quality, 58–60, 62–63
video storage, 61
video-sharing feedback, 57–58, 66–68
video-sharing website, xiv, 57–58, 63–66, 68–69
viewing videos: of self / of others, 2, 4–7, 9, 15, 19, 29, 33

About the Contributors

Alex Chambers, PhD, is currently assistant professor at William Patterson University of New Jersey in the Department of Special Education and Counseling. He has a great deal of experience using technology to enhance online instruction. His research interests include assessment, multicultural curriculum development, transition, self-advocacy, and using technology in instruction. His research has focused on providing self-advocacy instruction to culturally and linguistically diverse populations, as well as web-based reading interventions. He is the author of peer-reviewed articles and book chapters in the areas of self-advocacy and inclusion.

Michelle Gonzalez, PhD, is assistant professor at William Paterson University of New Jersey. She teaches a variety of literacy courses and supervises in the university reading clinic where teachers are trained for certification as reading specialists. Dr. Gonzalez has published and presented widely on the topics of universal design for learning in K–12 and postsecondary settings, technology integration in the early childhood classroom, and best practices in literacy and teacher education.

Joan Roman, MEd, is Manager of Grants and Compliance for a system of charter schools in both North Carolina and South Carolina. She was the founding principal of two charter schools for this network and blazed the trail for the educational management company within the state of North Carolina. She has in-depth experience in fostering instructional practices that drive individual student achievement in reading, math, and science. Her research on struggling readers, intensive small-group instruction, and the utilization of modeling metacognitive strategies led to the high performance of the charter schools she opened.

About the Editors

Carrie Eunyoung Hong, PhD, is professor of literacy at William Paterson University of New Jersey. She directs the Masters of Education in Literacy Program in which classroom teachers are trained to be certified reading specialists. She has extensive experience directing federal and state grant programs that provide professional development for teachers. Her research interests include reading, writing, balanced literacy, literacy teacher education, and teacher preparation for working with culturally and linguistically diverse learners. She is the author of refereed articles and book chapters in the area of teacher education and professional development.

Irene Van Riper, EdD, is assistant professor at West Liberty University in West Virginia. She was instrumental in developing the Reading Specialist courses in the MAED program at West Liberty University. She has in-depth experience in teacher preparation for reading specialists and teachers of individuals with disabilities. Her research projects, professional development programs, and publications mark her expertise in dyslexia, autism spectrum disorders, and reading education. She has earned associate-level certification from the Academy of Orton-Gillingham Practitioners and Educators. She is the author of peer-reviewed articles and book chapters and the editor of books in the areas of teacher education and special education.

www.ingramcontent.com/pod-product-compliance
Lightning Source LLC
Chambersburg PA
CBHW032031230426
43671CB00005B/277